THE
O. J. SIMPSON
MURDER TRIAL

A Headline Court Case

Headline Court Cases

The Trial of Gangster Al Capone
A Headline Court Case
0-7660-1482-7

The Alger Hiss Communist Spy Trial
A Headline Court Case
0-7660-1483-5

The Andersonville Prison Civil War Crimes Trial
A Headline Court Case
0-7660-1386-3

The Court-Martial Trial of West Point Cadet Johnson Whittaker
A Headline Court Case
0-7660-1485-1

The John Brown Slavery Revolt Trial
A Headline Court Case
0-7660-1385-5

The Lindbergh Baby Kidnapping Trial
A Headline Court Case
0-7660-1389-8

The Lizzie Borden "Axe Murder" Trial
A Headline Court Case
0-7660-1422-3

The Mary Surratt "Lincoln Assassination" Trial
A Headline Court Case
0-7660-1481-9

The Nuremberg Nazi War Crimes Trials
A Headline Court Case
0-7660-1384-7

The O. J. Simpson Murder Trial
A Headline Court Case
0-7660-1480-0

The Rosenberg Cold War Spy Trial
A Headline Court Case
0-7660-1479-7

The Sacco and Vanzetti Controversial Murder Trial
A Headline Court Case
0-7660-1387-1

The Salem Witchcraft Trials
A Headline Court Case
0-7660-1383-9

The Scopes Monkey Trial
A Headline Court Case
0-7660-1338-X

The Teapot Dome Scandal Trial
A Headline Court Case
0-7660-1484-3

THE O. J. SIMPSON MURDER TRIAL

A Headline Court Case

Michael J. Pellowski

Enslow Publishers, Inc.

40 Industrial Road   PO Box 38
Box 398   Aldershot
Berkeley Heights, NJ 07922   Hants GU12 6BP
USA   UK

http://www.enslow.com

To Howard and Audrey Snyder

Library of Congress Cataloging-in-Publication Data

Pellowski, Michael J.
The O.J. Simpson murder trial : a headline court case / Michael J.
Pellowski.
      p. cm. – (Headline court cases)
Includes bibliographical references and index.
ISBN 0-7660-1480-0
1. Simpson, O. J., 1947—Trials, litigation, etc.—Juvenile literature. 2. Trials (Murder)—
California—Los Angeles—Juvenile literature. 3. Murder—California—Los Angeles—
Investigation—Juvenile literature. 4. Simpson, Nicole Brown, d. 1994—Juvenile literature.
5. Goldman, Ronald Lyle, 1968-1994—Juvenile literature. I. Title. II. Series.
KF224.S485 P45 2001
345.73'02523'0979494—dc21
      00-011907

Printed in the United States of America

10 9 8 7 6 5 4 3 2

To Our Readers:
We have done our best to make sure all Internet addresses in this book were active and appropriate
when we went to press. However, the author and the publisher have no control over and assume no
liability for the material available on those Internet sites or on other Web sites they may link to. Any
comments or suggestions can be sent by e-mail to comments@enslow.com or to the address on the
back cover.

Photo Credits: CNP/Steve Grayson/Pool/Archive Photos, p. 46; Darlene Hammond/
Archive Photos, p. 18; Express Newspapers/0002/Archive Photos, p. 50; Fotos
International/A Horvathova/Archive Photos, p. 85; Lee/Archive Photos, p. 23; Lynne
Lucke/Archive Photos, pp. 3, 21, 57; Popperfoto/Archive Photos, p. 15; Reuters/Archive
Photos, p. 62; Reuters/Mike Nelson/Archive Photos, p. 71; Reuters/Mike Segar/Archive
Photos, p. 33; Reuters/Myung J. Chun/Archive Photos, p. 42; Reuters/Sam
Mircovich/Archive Photos, pp. 34, 37, 38, 44, 59, 76, 94; Reuters/Steve Grayson/Archive
Photos, p. 53; Reuters/Stringer/Archive Photos, p. 27; Sonia Moskowitz/Archive Photos,
p. 9; Sporting News/Archive Photos, p. 17.

Cover Photo: Reuters/Sam Mircovich/Archive Photos (background); Popperfoto/
Archive Photos (inset).

Contents

chapter one

A DATE WITH DEATH

LOS ANGELES—At 10:15 on the night of June 12, 1994, Pablo Fenjves, one of Nicole Brown Simpson's neighbors, heard what he later described to officers with the Los Angeles Police Department (LAPD) as "a dog's plaintive wail."[1]

Forty minutes later that same neighbor found Brown Simpson's pet Akita, Kato, as the disoriented dog wandered aimlessly around the Brentwood, California, condominium complex where she lived. The normally well-groomed pet was a horrifying sight. Its paws were bloody and the dog seemed to be extremely agitated. However, the dog was not wounded or injured in any way. No one knew it at the time, but the blood soaking the dog's paws was human blood.

Another of Nicole Brown Simpson's concerned neighbors took the dog home, but the Akita refused to calm down. Nicole Brown Simpson's pet could not be comforted and finally the neighbors decided to release the disturbed animal. It was ten minutes past midnight on June 13, 1994. Once released, the dog led neighbors Sukru Boztepe and Bettina Rasmussen to a grisly discovery.

A Murder Is Discovered

Sprawled on the ground near a gate outside of Brown Simpson's condominium were the bloody, lifeless bodies of Nicole Brown Simpson and her friend Ron L. Goldman who worked as a waiter in a nearby restaurant. The bodies of Simpson and Goldman were punctured with what were later determined to be deep knife cuts. Neighbors quickly told the Los Angeles Police Department about their discovery.

Approximately four hours later, Nicole Brown Simpson's ex-husband checked into the O'Hare Plaza Hotel in Chicago, Illinois. The murdered woman's ex-husband was O. J. Simpson, the former star running back for the Buffalo Bills of the National Football League (NFL) and a Hollywood celebrity. Orenthal James "O. J." Simpson also lived in California, not far from the scene of the crime, but had flown to Chicago to participate in a promotional golf tournament.

The same night that the bodies of Nicole Brown Simpson and Ron Goldman were found, O. J. Simpson had seen his ex-wife at their daughter Sydney's dance recital. Nicole and O. J. had gone through a series of arguments before deciding to divorce and live apart. O. J. Simpson was known to have a hidden, dark side to his lively on-screen personality. On earlier occasions Nicole Brown Simpson

Orenthal James "O. J." Simpson, former star running back for the NFL's Buffalo Bills, Hollywood celebrity, and former husband of Nicole Brown Simpson, is shown here.

had contacted the police to file charges of harassment and physical abuse against her then-husband.[2]

O. J. Simpson was known by friends to be extremely possessive of his ex-wife. He was known to be jealous of her male acquaintances. In reality, O. J. Simpson was not always like the happy, easy-going characters he portrayed in movies and in television commercials.

Off the Record

"Everyone sees this golden hero, or golden nice guy, but I have my faults too," O. J. Simpson revealed in an interview for the *San Francisco Examiner* in March 1978.[3]

But could O. J. Simpson's self-confessed faults make him capable of committing murder? At first, he was not a suspect in the murders. When the Los Angeles Police Department contacted him at 6:00 A.M. in Chicago, it was only to inform him of his ex-wife's death.

Immediately, Simpson checked out of his hotel and returned to his Brentwood, California, mansion. By the time O. J. Simpson arrived in Brentwood, at approximately 11:30 A.M., on June 13, 1994, officers with the Los Angeles Police Department had gathered what they felt was significant evidence against Simpson. They believed that Simpson himself had committed the murders before leaving for Chicago.

Detectives from the LAPD confronted Simpson and advised him of his rights. Handcuffs were placed on the popular celebrity and former NFL great. O. J. Simpson instantly declared his innocence. Minutes later, celebrity attorney Howard Weitzman arrived and had the cuffs removed, but Simpson was not a free man. Many unanswered questions remained.

Simpson was taken away and questioned thoroughly by police for three hours. At the end of the questioning, no arrest was made. Nevertheless, the controversial and sometimes bizarre case of the O. J. Simpson murder trial had begun. It would not end until over a year later.

chapter two

A FAMOUS SUSPECT

BEFORE THE CRIME—It is a known fact that crime stories help sell more newspapers than any other type of news story.[1] Thus, the deaths of Nicole Brown Simpson and Ron Goldman quickly caught the attention of the national press. If the person Los Angeles police detectives first questioned about the crime had been ordinary, just any everyday individual, public interest about the case might have quickly and quietly peaked and then disappeared. However, the son of Jimmy and Eunice Simpson was well known to the world as O. J.—the Juice—a former pro football star and a Hollywood celebrity.

"When you remove him [O. J. Simpson] from the equation there is simply no way that this case could be considered an unusual or exceptional murder case," said Vincent Bugliosi, the former Los Angeles prosecutor.[2]

"However, add to the crime mix that the murder victims were white and O. J. Simpson is an Afro-American and you have all the right elements of an explosive, best-selling story certain to enthrall a nation of newspaper readers and TV viewers for months and perhaps years."[3]

News of O. J. Simpson's possible connection to the crime opened a floodgate of questions. Cries of racial bias, prejudice, and sloppy police work quickly had people all over the United States choosing sides in the question of O. J. Simpson's guilt or innocence. O. J. Simpson is black and both of the murder victims were white. These facts polarized many blacks and whites against each other.

Headlines asked: Did O. J. do it? Was O. J. lying? Is O. J. innocent? In a case where there was no eyewitness, no recovered murder weapon, and tainted evidence that may or may not have been conclusive, the American public chose to form its own pretrial judgments. Those judgments often tended to be based on race rather than on facts.

At the start of what may have been the most famous court case of the 1990s, people all over America and the world looked at O. J. Simpson and came to their own conclusions about his guilt or innocence. Many asked an important question: Was justice truly served in the O. J. Simpson trial? Different people had very different answers to this question.

Who Is O. J. Simpson?

Orenthal James Simpson was born on July 9, 1947, to Jimmy Simpson and Eunice Durden Simpson in San Francisco, California. He was the third of four children in a poor family. He grew up in California and played high school football at Galileo High School in San Francisco. As a young boy, O. J. was popular and friendly and always knew how to make friends. When he was young he would stand outside the gates of a San Francisco 49ers football game and talk soft-hearted fans into giving him their extra tickets. Then the young Simpson would turn around and sell those tickets to other football fans, and make a profit.[4]

A Football Hero

After playing football for two years at City College of San Francisco, O. J. Simpson went to the University of Southern California on a football scholarship. As a running back, Simpson was an All-American in 1967 and in 1968. In 1968, Simpson also won the Heisman Trophy as the nation's outstanding college football player.

Simpson was drafted by the NFL's Buffalo Bills and led the league in rushing in 1972. In 1973 he became the first NFL running back to rush for more than 2,000 yards in a single season. He was rewarded for his accomplishments when he was named the Associated Press Athlete of the Year.

The All-Pro running back played for the Buffalo Bills until 1977 and finished his NFL career playing for the San Francisco 49ers in 1978 and 1979.

Simpson gained 3,124 yards in college and scored 33 touchdowns. In the NFL, he rushed for 11,236 yards and tallied 61 touchdowns in the course of his career. He is a member of the College Football Hall of Fame and the Professional Football Hall of Fame.[5]

O. J. Simpson won the Heisman Trophy as the nation's outstanding college football player in 1968.

Movie Star

After retiring from professional football in 1980, O. J. Simpson easily made a transition from the world of sports to the world of show business. He worked as a sports announcer and analyst. He also appeared in television commercials. He later was featured in a series of *Naked Gun* movies. His fame as a movie star and celebrity always kept him in the public eye. His warm and friendly on-screen personality made him a favorite with fans.

O. J. Simpson—Husband and Father

O. J. Simpson married Marguerite Whitley, his high school sweetheart, on June 24, 1967. They had three children—Arnelle (the oldest daughter), Jason Lamar (a son) and daughter Aaren—in their eleven-year marriage. Tragically, Aaren was only twenty-three months old when she died in a swimming pool accident in 1979. It was during that same year that the marriage ended. By the time of O. J.'s divorce from Marguerite, he was already deep into a new relationship with young Nicole Brown.

Nicole Brown Simpson

Nicole Brown was an eighteen-year-old waitress at a Beverly Hills nightclub called The Daisy when she met O. J. Simpson. Simpson was thirty. They quickly hit it off and began dating. Simpson and Brown were married on February 2, 1985. They had a daughter, Sydney, and then a son, Justin.

The marriage had some disturbing moments sprinkled

When he retired from professional football in 1980, O. J. Simpson became a sports commentator and later, a Hollywood movie star.

O. J. Simpson and Nicole Brown Simpson are shown here with their children Sydney (front row, middle) and Justin (front row, left).

among the many good times. O. J. Simpson was known to have a temper and was extremely jealous of the attention his wife received from other men.[6]

On New Year's Day 1989, O. J. and Nicole had a huge fight. The police photographed a battered Nicole and an official report was filed about the incident. At the time, referring to O.J. Simpson, Nicole told police, "He's going to kill me!"[7]

O. J. Simpson pleaded guilty to a wife beating charge and agreed to perform community service and attend counseling. He later dismissed the incident by saying it was "no big deal."[8]

In 1992 the marriage ended in divorce. The court awarded O. J. and Nicole joint custody of Sydney and Justin. As parents, they continued to live close to each other in California and were frequently together at events and activities involving their children. O. J. still cared for Nicole and could not stay away from his ex-wife, at times even stalking her.[9]

"Well, we tried to get back together, and it just didn't work. It wasn't working and so we were going our separate ways." said O. J. Simpson.[10]

In October 1993, O. J. Simpson's rage erupted again and was directed at his ex-wife Nicole. The incident occurred eight months before the slayings of Nicole Brown Simpson and Ron Goldman and was recorded on a 911 tape. O. J. Simpson kicked at Nicole Brown Simpson's door and an argument started. Brown Simpson pleaded with her former spouse to quiet down because the children were sleeping.

O. J. Simpson accused Nicole Brown Simpson of failing to think of her children on a recent occasion when she had been with another man.

The real O. J. Simpson was never an easy man to truly know. He had a public face and a very different private face. In a 1974 interview he described himself as totally nonviolent. "I'm not violent . . . even on the football field I try to avoid contact. I try not to hit anybody or let them hit me."[11]

Who was and is the real O. J. Simpson? That question has not been answered to the satisfaction of many people interested in the case and perhaps it never will be.

After his divorce, O. J. Simpson began dating a new girlfriend, Paula Barbieri. He was with Barbieri the day before his daughter's dance recital. He did not bring Barbieri with him to the recital, however. At the recital, Simpson's ex-wife Nicole ignored him.

Did those events somehow trigger another rage response in O. J. Simpson? Or was Simpson an innocent pawn in a plot to frame him for murder? The events leading up to the crime could neither confirm nor refute Simpson's possible role in the dual murders.

A Murderous Timetable?

The events before the killing of Nicole Brown Simpson and Ron Goldman, the crime itself, and what happened after the murders were all carefully documented by the Los Angeles Police Department in an approximate timetable.

O. J. Simpson and his ex-wife Nicole Brown Simpson both attended their nine-year-old daughter Sydney's dance recital at Paul Revere Junior High School in California, leaving at about 6:00 P.M. on Sunday, June 12, 1994.

After the recital, Nicole Brown Simpson had dinner with family and friends at Mezzaluna, a neighborhood restaurant where Ron Goldman worked as a waiter. Goldman was on duty when Nicole Brown Simpson's group arrived around 6:30 P.M., but he did not wait on their table.

Meanwhile, at O. J. Simpson's nearby Brentwood estate, Brian "Kato" Kaelin, a resident at Simpson's guesthouse, saw and talked to Simpson between 6:30 and 7:00 P.M. The time was determined by the fact that the NBA playoff game

After his divorce from Nicole, O. J. Simpson began dating Paula Barbieri. Simpson and Barbieri are shown here in 1993.

between the Houston Rockets and the New York Knicks, which Kaelin had been watching on television, had just ended.

At 8:30 P.M. Kaelin went to his room to make a phone call. At the same time, at Mezzaluna, Nicole Brown Simpson was just leaving for home.

O. J. Simpson and Kato Kaelin got together to go out for food at 9:10 P.M. They took Simpson's Rolls Royce and went through a McDonald's drive through sometime between 9:22 and 9:25 P.M.

A woman who had dined with Nicole Brown Simpson at Mezzaluna discovered someone had left behind a pair of prescription sunglasses at the table. She asked that they be put in an envelope so they could be returned if someone called to ask about them. It was 9:30 P.M. At 9:35 P.M., Nicole Brown Simpson called the restaurant to ask about the glasses. Her friend Ron Goldman agreed to bring them to her home.

At O. J. Simpson's Brentwood estate, Simpson and Kaelin returned with fast food around 9:40 P.M. and went to separate places in the house to eat.

Ron Goldman left Mezzaluna at 9:50 P.M. with Nicole Brown Simpson's prescription glasses.

Sometime between 10:15 P.M. and 10:20 P.M., one of Nicole Brown Simpson's neighbors heard the agitated barking of Brown Simpson's dog.

In Brentwood, a limousine driver named Allan Park arrived at O. J. Simpson's estate at 10:25 P.M., earlier than scheduled, to drive Simpson to the airport. Simpson was

Brian "Kato" Kaelin was a resident at O. J. Simpson's guesthouse at the time of the murders of Nicole Brown Simpson and Ron Goldman. He spent time with O. J. Simpson on the night of the murders.

flying to Chicago. Park did not see O. J. Simpson's white Bronco parked in the street when he arrived. He remained at a gate of the estate and waited. At 10:40 P.M., Allan Park buzzed the house intercom to tell Simpson he had arrived. No one answered his call. He buzzed repeatedly from 10:40 P.M. until 10:50 P.M.

Meanwhile, Kato Kaelin was on the phone in the guesthouse. He heard odd noises outside and went out to investigate. He saw the limousine parked outside the gate and continued around the house to check out the noises. Allan Park decided to page his boss to ask what to do. At 10:55 P.M. Park's boss returned his page and told him to continue to wait for Simpson.

A neighbor of Nicole Brown Simpson's was walking a dog near her home at 10:55 P.M. He found Brown Simpson's disoriented dog wandering around. The dog's paws were soaked with blood.

Meanwhile, back at O. J. Simpson's estate, Allan Park was still waiting. It was between 10:56 and 10:57 P.M. While watching the estate, Park saw a white male with a flashlight. (It was Kato Kaelin investigating the noise he had heard from inside.) At the same time, the limo driver saw a black person who was about six feet tall and two hundred pounds and wearing dark clothing cross the driveway and enter the house. Allan Park was unsure of the mysterious individual's gender or identity. Kaelin then approached Park. Kaelin asked the driver if O. J. might have overslept. Park buzzed the house again and someone finally answered. A voice said he would be out shortly. Lights went on in the house and O. J. Simpson came out. It was 11:00 P.M.

Allan Park, Kato Kaelin, and O. J. Simpson loaded bags into the limo until 11:15 P.M. Park then drove Simpson to the airport, arriving at 11:35 P.M. At 11:45 O. J. Simpson flew to Chicago.

Just past midnight on June 13, 1994, Nicole Brown Simpson's dog led her neighbors to the bloody murder scene. Nicole Brown Simpson and Ron Goldman were found dead at 12:10 A.M.

Evidence of a Crime

Early in the morning on June 13, 1994, O. J. Simpson was in O'Hare Plaza Hotel in Chicago as Los Angeles police detectives began their investigation into the double murder. The police were not yet sure where O. J. Simpson was. They went to his Brentwood estate, hoping to find him so they could notify him of the death of his ex-wife. (O. J. Simpson's defense attorneys would later question the reason for the trip to the house.)

At that point the police had little information about the murders. There was no murder weapon. There seemed to be no motive for the crime. The only things police had were some bloody footprints, one bloody glove, and a wool cap that were discovered at the murder scene.

The police steadfastly insist their intent in going to O. J. Simpson's estate was to inform him of the murder of Nicole Brown Simpson. The estate was only two miles from the murder scene. It is fenced in and protected by a security service.

At the estate, the police saw blood stains on O. J. Simpson's white Ford Bronco parked in the street. A trail of blood led from the Bronco toward the house.

When police detectives Mark Fuhrman and Philip Vannatter arrived at the scene, they saw several vehicles in the fenced driveway and a light on in the house. They believed someone was in the house, but did not know who it might be. Fuhrman and Vannatter examined the blood on the Bronco and the trail of blood drops leading to the house. The police contacted Westec Security, the company that protected the Simpson residence. Westec sent a vehicle to the location and also gave the officers the telephone number inside Simpson's house. The police phoned the house and got an answering machine.

An Emergency or a Plot?

The detectives claimed, based on the blood stains outside, that they felt an emergency situation existed. Detective Mark Fuhrman jumped over the security fence. Others followed and went in search of people in the house. They went to the guest quarters of Brian "Kato" Kaelin and woke him up. The officers (knowing there were bloody footprints at the crime scene) checked Kaelin's tennis shoes. There were no traces of blood on his shoes. Kaelin was then asked who else was at the estate. Kaelin directed the police to the guest quarters of Simpson's daughter from his first marriage, Arnelle.

Arnelle Simpson took the police to the main house and used her key to open the front door. Westec Security had informed the police that O. J. Simpson had a live-in maid, Gigi Guarin. The officers went to her room, but she was not there. The maid had the day off. Arrangements were then made with Arnelle to have the Simpson children (Sydney and Justin), who were at a local police station, taken care of.

Finally, O. J. Simpson was located with the help of his secretary, Cathy Rand. The police contacted him at his hotel in Chicago. Nicole's parents and friends of O. J. Simpson's were also contacted. The friends included O. J.'s old pro football buddy Al Cowlings.

When police arrived at O. J. Simpson's estate to tell him about the murder of Nicole Brown Simpson, they discovered blood stains on his white Ford Bronco.

Police Work

The police were at O. J. Simpson's estate without a search warrant, but at no time did anyone ask them to leave. (This was a legal point raised later in the trial.) Kato Kaelin told the officers about the noises he had heard earlier. Detective Mark Fuhrman walked down a path and made a startling discovery. In an area of the dark path leading to the south gate, near an air conditioner, Fuhrman found a bloody glove. The glove appeared to be the mate to the glove found at the murder scene. Detective Fuhrman did not explore any other areas of the Simpson property. He then took other detectives, one at a time, to the location of the second glove.

In Chicago, O. J. Simpson checked out of his hotel and booked a flight home. In California, Dennis Fung, a criminologist for the Los Angeles Police Department arrived at the Simpson estate. A criminologist is a police scientist who gathers clues and evidence from a crime scene, and later analyzes the clues and evidence.

He sealed off key areas with yellow crime tape and covered blood drops with paper cups. Other officers helped secure the estate while a judge issued a search warrant. A case was being built against O. J. Simpson.

chapter three

O. J. SIMPSON ACCUSED AND PURSUED

INVESTIGATION—When O. J. Simpson arrived at his Brentwood, California, mansion around 11:00 A.M. on Monday, June 13, 1994, the police were there waiting for him. Using a search warrant to gain access to his house and his vehicle, detectives found more blood in various areas of Simpson's house and also in his vehicle, a Ford Bronco. Circumstantial evidence, evidence that seems to point to a conclusion but is not concrete, was mounting against O. J. Simpson. The police believed they had a case against Simpson.

When Simpson arrived home, he was handcuffed but he was not placed under arrest. His lawyer and friend, Howard Weitzman, had the police remove the handcuffs before Simpson was taken away for questioning about the murders.

O. J. Simpson Is Questioned

Police detectives Philip Vannatter and Thomas Lange carefully questioned O. J. Simpson for about three hours. Before answering any questions, O. J. Simpson was advised of his rights. He was told he had the right to remain silent, he had a right to have a lawyer present, and that anything he did say would be used against him in a court of law.

Simpson gave up the right to remain silent and the right to have an attorney present. The police advised Simpson they were investigating the death of his ex-wife and another man. They questioned Simpson about his relationship with Nicole Brown Simpson during their marriage and after their divorce. Simpson was calm and cooperative. He stated during the beginning of the interview that being apart from Nicole was not easy for him. "For me, it was big problems. I loved her, I didn't want us to separate," admitted Simpson.[1]

When the questioning turned to Simpson's white Bronco parked outside of his estate, he explained that the Hertz (Rent-a-Car) Company owned the Bronco, but it had been given to him to use. He, the housekeeper, and others at the estate often used it, and it was normally parked on the street.

The police also questioned Simpson about his daughter's recital, the last time he saw Nicole, and the things he did before leaving for Chicago. Then the detectives turned their attention to an injury; a cut on O. J. Simpson's hand. Simpson did not know how he had first injured his hand, but he claimed he had reopened the cut at the hotel in Chicago when the police phoned him to give him the news of Nicole's death. In a state of distress, he claimed, he had broken a glass.

Detective Thomas Lange asked, "Do you recall bleeding at all in your truck, in the Bronco?"

O. J. Simpson answered, "I recall bleeding at my house, and then I went to the Bronco. The last thing I did before I left when I was rushing, was went and got my phone out of the Bronco."[2]

He further explained that he often suffered cuts from playing golf and other things. Simpson also insisted that he had been on good terms with Nicole before leaving for Chicago. In addition, he revealed he had worn tennis shoes (Reebok sneakers) the night of Sydney's recital. He also admitted he had cut his hand somehow on the night of the recital but did not know how. He understood at that early stage his status as the ex-husband of one of the murder victims made him a possible suspect.

Near the end of the questioning, Simpson said to detective Thomas Lange, "I know I'm the number one target, and now you tell me I've got blood all over the place."[3]

A photographer was then summoned to take a picture of the cut on O. J. Simpson's hand. The first interview ended shortly after a discussion about a polygraph test. Also known as a lie detector test, a polygraph measures a person's uncontrollable emotional responses to questions in order to determine whether that person is telling the truth. It is not, however, foolproof. Simpson said he would consider taking a polygraph test since it might eliminate him as a suspect. "If it's true blue, I don't mind taking it," said Simpson.[4]

Free, But Under Suspicion

After being questioned by the police, O. J. Simpson was released. No official charges were filed against him. The following day, Tuesday, June 14, 1994, the tide of circumstantial evidence began to turn against O. J. Simpson. Police seized clothing and other belongings from Simpson's estate. The police also began tests on the blood found at the scene of the crime, at Simpson's estate, and in his Bronco. The coroner's office released an initial report.

News stories indicated that the bloodstains found in O. J. Simpson's vehicle and in his driveway matched types discovered at the crime scene. An examination of the bodies of Nicole Brown Simpson and Ron Goldman indicated the victims had died as a result of sharp force injuries. (They had most likely been stabbed to death with a knife.)

O. J. Simpson's Ford Bronco and a pair of his sneakers were confiscated. Rumors also circulated that a bloody glove was discovered at Simpson's estate.

Simpson's attorney, Howard Weitzman, initially issued a disclaimer to the rumor. Said Weitzman in an interview, "I have been told by law enforcement that there was no bloody glove found at Mr. Simpson's residence."[5]

A short time later, Howard Weitzman bowed out as O. J. Simpson's lawyer in the case, citing a close personal relationship with his client. High-profile attorney Robert Shapiro would take over.

Police sources then confirmed that blood at the crime scene matched the blood found at O. J. Simpson's estate. The police watched Simpson more carefully even as his attorney loudly professed his client's innocence. "At the time that this murder took place, O. J. was at home waiting to get into a limousine to take him to the airport on a trip that had been planned well in advance for a promotional event in Chicago," attorney Robert Shapiro told the press.[6]

The police would neither confirm nor deny that O. J. Simpson was a suspect in the double murder. They were playing a waiting game. During that time, a strange thing happened. O. J. Simpson's Ford Bronco was broken into while in police custody at a towing service. Souvenir hunters were thought to be responsible, but no one knew for certain.

Meanwhile, O. J. Simpson was quietly spending time with his children Sydney and Justin. On June 15, he attended the viewing for his ex-wife Nicole. On June 16, he accompanied his children to their mother's funeral in Brentwood, California. O. J. Simpson appeared to the public to be a grieving ex-husband concerned about the future welfare of his young children. The police, however, were forming a different picture of O. J. Simpson.

Police in Chicago searched a field near the hotel where O. J. Simpson had stayed on the night of the murders. They were looking for a possible murder weapon. A man fitting

Members of the Los Angeles Police Department were busy building a case against O. J. Simpson after it was confirmed that the blood at the crime scene matched the blood found at Simpson's estate.

On June 16, 1994, O. J. Simpson accompanied his children, Sydney (left) and Justin (right), to their mother's funeral.

Simpson's description had been seen in the field. The search in Chicago turned up no new evidence, but the Los Angeles district attorney was almost ready to act.

Flight From Arrest

On Friday, June 17, 1994, O. J. Simpson was charged with two counts of murder with special circumstances. Two counts referred to the fact that two people had been killed. Special circumstances referred to the fact that one of the murders (that of Nicole Brown Simpson) may have been planned in advance. Prosecutors said they might seek the death penalty in the case.

Simpson had been staying at the home of his friend Robert Kardashian located in Encino, California. Robert Shapiro, Simpson's attorney, had arranged with the LAPD to have him voluntarily surrender at 11:00 A.M. at police headquarters.

When Simpson failed to appear at police headquarters as planned, police phoned Robert Shapiro. They informed the attorney that officers would arrive shortly at Kardashian's house to take Simpson into custody. When the officers arrived shortly after noon, Simpson was gone. He had left with his friend Al Cowlings in a white Ford Bronco similar to the one Simpson had. A so-called suicide note written by Simpson was left behind. The note read, in part:

> To Whom It May Concern:
>
> First, everyone understand I had nothing to do with Nicole's murder. I loved her, always have and always will. If we had a problem, it's because I loved her so much.

It was tough splitting . . . but we both knew it was for the best. Inside I had no doubt that in the future we would be close friends or more. Unlike what has been written in the press, Nicole and I had a great relationship for most of our lives together. Like all long-term relationships we had a few downs and ups.

I'm sorry for the Goldman family. I know how much it hurts.

Don't feel sorry for me. I've had a great life, great friends. Please think of the real O. J. and not this lost person. Thanks for making my life special. I hope I helped yours.

Peace and Love,

O. J.[7]

The Chase

At approximately 6:45 on the evening of June 17, 1994, O. J. Simpson was spotted by police on the expressway in a white Ford Bronco driven by his friend Al Cowlings.

A wild chase that was televised live from helicopters above began through Southern Los Angeles. Police cars lined up and pursued the white Bronco, which moved at a moderate speed up and down the California freeway. Simpson reportedly had a gun and Al Cowlings used a cell phone to alert police that Simpson was considering suicide. Photos of Simpson showed him pressing a gun to his head. The LAPD cautiously continued to trail the murder suspect but did not close in on the vehicle.

Along the route of the Bronco, crowds gathered. Some people booed as the white Bronco passed. Others who believed Simpson to be innocent cheered and urged him on. It was one of the most bizarre police episodes in American history. It continued for hours as American and world viewers watched the wild chase live on television.

At 8:00 P.M., the Bronco driven by Cowlings turned into Simpson's Brentwood mansion. There was a brief standoff before negotiations began.

Simpson finally surrendered to police officers at 8:51 P.M. He was clutching a family photo when he was taken into custody and jailed without bail.

When the police seized Cowlings' Bronco, they found O. J. Simpson's passport and a disguise consisting of a fake goatee (beard) and moustache. Al Cowlings also had $8,750 in cash in his pocket, which he told detectives Simpson had given to him while they were in the Bronco. The detectives

A Ford Bronco carrying O. J. Simpson (hidden in the back seat) is driven by Al Cowlings, Simpson's former teammate.

A man cheers as O. J. Simpson's Bronco comes down the freeway.

then made a mistake and booked the cash as Cowlings' personal property and not as evidence. That mistake would later prove damaging to the prosecution, because it would be difficult to prove that O. J. Simpson had planned the crime and his escape ahead of time.

Does a person carrying a passport, a disguise, and almost $9,000 in cash appear suicidal, or is that person about to flee the country? Prosecutors would not be able to pose that question because the cash had been logged in by police as Al Cowlings' personal property.

Other items found in Cowlings' vehicle were a bottle of spirit gum to make the goatee and moustache stick and adhesive remover to get them off. The disguise had been purchased from Cinema Secrets Beauty Supply in Burbank, California. There was a receipt for the purchase dated May 27, 1994.[8]

The disguise had been purchased more than two weeks before the murders. That seemed inconsequential at the time, but it later supported a wild theory posed by one of Nicole Brown Simpson's friends, Faye Resnick. The Los Angeles district attorney chose not to introduce Resnick's theory in court, but Resnick believed O. J. Simpson murdered Nicole Brown Simpson after planning it ahead of time. She believed Simpson had, in fact, planned his wife's murder for some time. (Ron Goldman, apparently, just happened to be in the wrong place at the wrong time.) The O. J. Simpson murder case was quickly becoming more and more baffling.

A Preliminary Hearing

A preliminary hearing, a hearing to determine whether there is enough evidence for a trial, was held from June 30 to July 8, 1994. The hearing was presided over by municipal judge Kathleen Kennedy-Powell.

When the district attorney presented evidence linking O. J. Simpson to the murders, a major conflict erupted at the hearing over hair samples. A navy blue knit cap had been discovered at the murder scene. In the cap were hairs from an African-American male. The prosecutors wanted hair samples from O. J. Simpson's head to determine if his hair matched the samples found in the cap. Simpson did, eventually, donate hair samples, but the number of hairs he would agree to donate became a major issue.

Other evidence included the bloody glove found at the Simpson home and blood samples from the victims (Nicole Brown Simpson and Ron Goldman) found at the crime scene and at Simpson's estate.

A knife purchased by O. J. Simpson from Ross Cutlery close to the time of the murders and a knife later discovered in Simpson's home became another matter for debate. However, DNA testing, tests used to determine a person's blood type, along with Simpson's history of abusing his ex-wife and the glove found outside O. J. Simpson's home (which appeared to have the blood of the victims and Simpson's blood on it) worked in favor of the prosecuting team.

After a six-day hearing, Judge Kennedy-Powell ruled there was enough evidence to put O. J. Simpson on trial for the murders of Nicole Brown Simpson and Ron Goldman.

chapter four

THE CRIMINAL TRIAL BEGINS

COURTROOM—On July 22, 1994, O. J. Simpson stood at his arraignment before supervisory criminal court judge Cecil Mills. In an arraignment, the accused person is summoned to court to plead guilty or not guilty to the charges. Judge Mills looked at O. J. Simpson and asked, "How do you plead?"

"Absolutely, one hundred percent, not guilty!" answered O. J. Simpson.

O. J. Simpson steadfastly professed his innocence. In fact, before the arraignment, Simpson had offered a $500,000 reward for information leading to the arrest of the "real" killer or killers of his ex-wife Nicole and Ron Goldman.

On the surface, O. J. Simpson's intentions in offering a reward seemed pure. However, the public was not always aware of all of Simpson's responses to details about the crime. For example, when police reached Simpson in Chicago on June 13, 1994, right after the murders, a detective told him his ex-wife had been killed. At first he was hysterical. Then it occurred to the detective that Simpson had never asked *which* ex-wife had been murdered. (He had been married once before he and Nicole were married.) He also never asked how she had been killed or by whom.[1]

Was O. J. Simpson innocent or guilty? The verdict would be decided in a court of law. The stage was set for a powerful legal drama and there were many star players in the cast for both sides.

The Prosecutors

The prosecuting team put together by Los Angeles District Attorney Gil Garcetti consisted of Marcia Clark, Bill

Marcia Clark (far left) and Christopher Darden (second from left) were part of the team of lawyers that was trying to prove that O. J. Simpson was guilty.

Hodgman, Scott Gordon, Alan Yochelson, Christopher Darden, and others.

Marcia Clark had been a deputy district attorney for Los Angeles County for fourteen years at the time of the trial. Some considered her the lead prosecutor, but she was really a coprosecutor with long-time deputy district attorney Bill Hodgman. Clark was skilled in complex scientific evidence including DNA technology.

Christopher Darden, an African-American man, had risen through the ranks of the district attorney's office. His first assignment had been in 1981. He had been brought into the Simpson case to handle an investigation of Al Cowlings' part in Simpson's flight from custody.

The Defense Team

The group of attorneys selected to handle O. J. Simpson's defense was quickly nicknamed "The Dream Team" by the press. The Dream Team consisted of Robert Shapiro, Barry Scheck, Alan Dershowitz, F. Lee Bailey, Peter Neufeld, Gerald Uelmen, Johnnie Cochran, and others.

Robert Shapiro was a high-profile California attorney. He was a former prosecutor who was once an associate of the famous criminal lawyer Harry Weiss. Shapiro had represented Christian Brando, the son of actor Marlon Brando, in a murder trial. Brando had been found guilty, but Shapiro also had many other celebrity clients.

F. Lee Bailey was one of the most famous defense attorneys in America. He had defended Patty Hearst and the Boston Strangler.

Alan Dershowitz was a Harvard law professor with a brilliant legal mind. He had been involved with many high-profile cases.

Johnnie Cochran was the foremost African-American attorney in Los Angeles. He had worked in the district attorney's office and had once defended famous Black Panther Geronimo Pratt in a murder trial. Pratt was found guilty, but Cochran's effort in his defense was widely applauded. Johnnie Cochran was a man noted for his ability to calm racial distress. His practice had come to focus on racial abuses among the officers of the LAPD.

Johnnie Cochran (bending down to speak with O. J. Simpson who is seated) was one of the many lawyers trying to prove Simpson's innocence.

The Judge

As supervisory court judge, Cecil Mills assigned judges to try cases, much like a school principal decides which classes are to be taught by which teachers. He had a pool of six to nine judges to choose from to preside over the Simpson case. Mills assigned Judge Lance Ito to the case.

Ito was a former prosecutor (in the 1980s) who prided himself on always being politically correct. He was careful not to say or do things that might offend or anger anyone. As a judge, he wanted to be totally fair, but he also wanted to be well liked. The high publicity surrounding the case may have intimidated him slightly, perhaps causing him to allow more to pass in court than a stricter, more forceful judge might have allowed. He had been on the bench for seven years. In a strange twist, Lance Ito's wife had been a captain with the LAPD.

Other Players

Other people with key roles in the case were criminologist Dennis Fung, Andrea Mazzola, and Collin Yamauchi. Fung was in charge of collecting evidence at the crime scene and at O. J. Simpson's estate. Andrea Mazzola was Fung's assistant. She was a trainee at the time, with only four months of experience. Collin Yamauchi performed the initial testing of Simpson's blood.

Detectives with the LAPD were led by Tom Lange and Phil Vannatter. Detective Mark Fuhrman was also instrumental in the case.

Also deeply involved were the Brown and Goldman

Judge Lance Ito was the judge who presided over O. J. Simpson's criminal trial.

families, which included Lou and Juditha Brown (Nicole's parents), Denise Brown (Nicole's sister), Patti Goldman (Ron's stepmother), Kim Goldman (Ron's sister), and Fred Goldman (Ron's father), who sternly demanded justice for their slain son.

Reenacting the Murder

Deputy prosecutor Christopher Darden's possible scenario of how the crimes were committed paints a disturbing mental picture of a man unable to control his jealousy and anger. Darden believed the crimes may have been committed in the following manner:

A man dressed in black, wearing quiet rubber-soled shoes, stood outside of Nicole Brown Simpson's condo on Bundy Drive in Brentwood. He watched her from the shadows. When he rang the bell, she came out to open the security gate because the intercom was broken. She came out in bare feet as if expecting someone she knew. As the man waited with a knife in his hand, Nicole Brown Simpson's pet Akita came up. The dog did not create a fuss. Perhaps the pet recognized the visitor. Nicole Brown Simpson opened the gate.

The man came out of the shadows and hit Brown Simpson with a fist and then the knife handle. Then the knife's pointed end found its intended victim—four times striking Brown Simpson in the neck.

Unexpectedly, Ron Goldman innocently appeared on the scene. The man pulled Goldman inside the gate and lifted him to the left so the fence and shrubs cornered him. The attacker went after his surprised victim in a ferocious manner. Ron Goldman fought valiantly but to no avail. The knife slashed his throat.

Turning back to Nicole, the murderer grabbed her by the hair and ran the knife's blade across her neck. The Akita barked. The killer dropped one glove and his hat. Blood dripped from a wound on the murderer. He then escaped down an alley toward a parked vehicle, leaving behind bloody footprints.

Who was the killer? Prosecutor Chris Darden believed it to be O. J. Simpson.[2] But was it really?

The Victims

Dr. Irwin Golden, the coroner who examined the bodies of the victims, determined that the cause of death in both cases was sharp force injuries from some kind of knife or bladed instrument.

Nicole Brown Simpson was found at the foot of the stairs leading from her condo to the front gate. The gate was left open. She was curled up on her left side. She was wearing a black, backless dress and had on no shoes. Her arms, legs, and face were stained with blood. There was a large wound injury to her neck.

Ron Goldman was just inside the gate. He had been pushed backward and was slumped against the stump of a palm tree. He was wearing blue jeans and a cotton sweater. Near his foot was a white envelope containing a pair of sunglasses. Goldman had injuries to his neck, back, head, hands, and thighs.

The Jury

The jury for the O. J. Simpson trial was selected from a pool of one thousand people. People who said they would suffer financial or personal hardships were excused right away. The remaining 304 possible jurors were given a lengthy questionnaire to fill out before appearing before the judge for oral questioning.

Lawyers for the prosecution and the defense were allowed to excuse twenty possible jurors without giving any reasons. Others could be excused for reasons such as bias or knowledge of the case. In the end, twelve jurors and twelve alternates were selected. The selection process was not televised and the names of the jurors were kept secret throughout the trial.

During the jury selection process, Faye Resnick, a friend of Nicole's, stirred up members of the media by making strange allegations against O. J. Simpson on television, in newspaper interviews, and in other print media. Resnick claimed that O. J. Simpson had openly discussed his thoughts of murdering his ex-wife Nicole. Resnick published her allegations in a book that came out during the jury selection process. Resnick's questionable background, which included drug abuse, created quite a stir. Judge Ito feared the publicity might affect possible jurors and briefly halted the selection process. After many delays, the jury for the O. J. Simpson trial was finalized on December 8, 1994.

Of the twenty-four possible jurors (twelve jurors and twelve alternates), there were fifteen blacks, six whites, and three Hispanics. Ten jurors were eventually replaced by alternates over the many months of the trial. The twelve jurors who made the final decision in the O. J. murder trial had the following characteristics:

- Two jurors were college graduates.

- Not one juror read a newspaper regularly.

- All jurors were Democrats.

- Nine jurors lived in rented houses.

- Three jurors owned their own homes.

Faye Resnick, a friend of Nicole Brown Simpson's, is shown here. Resnick claimed that O. J. Simpson had openly discussed his thoughts of murdering his ex-wife.

- Five jurors said they or a family member had had a negative experience with law enforcement.

- Five jurors thought it acceptable to use force on other family members.

- Two jurors had supervisory or management responsibilities at work.

- Nine jurors thought O. J. Simpson was less likely to have murdered his wife because he was a football star.

- The jury that delivered the final verdict in the O. J. Simpson case was made up of one African-American man, one Hispanic man, two white women, and eight African-American women.

The makeup of the jury seemed to please the prosecution team. It could have challenged up to twenty of the possible jurors. Anyone it felt might be prejudiced in favor of O. J. Simpson could have been replaced. It was apparently satisfied, however, that the jurors chosen were open-minded enough to make decisions based on the evidence presented.

chapter five

THE CASE FOR THE PROSECUTION

"There was enough physical evidence in this case to convict O. J. Simpson twenty times over."[1]

—Marcia Clark

"There was a ton of evidence, an unreal amount of evidence."[2]

—Chris Darden

Prosecutors Marcia Clark, Christopher Darden, Scott Gordon, Bill Hodgman, and Alan Yochelson, believed that O. J. Simpson was guilty. They also sincerely believed that they (with the help of the LAPD) had collected more than enough substantially incriminating physical evidence to convict Orenthal James Simpson of the brutal double murder.

Because there were no eyewitnesses to the crime and O. J. Simpson had continually professed his innocence, the evidence would have to be overwhelming in order to convict him. The prosecutors felt that it was. However, O. J. Simpson's fame as an athlete and a celebrity and the question of racial bias would prove to be key factors in the case. Many thought that Simpson had been unfairly targeted as a suspect simply because he was African American. Many minorities strongly believed that African Americans, Hispanics, and other minorities were being unjustly targeted by the police and convicted simply because of the color of their skin—not because of what they did.

Physical and Emotional Harassment

Before opening statements in the Simpson trial began, Judge Lance Ito had an important decision to make. Would the

Prosecutors felt that O. J. Simpson's fame as an athlete and a celebrity would be key factors in the case.

prosecution be allowed to present evidence to the jury about O. J. Simpson's history of physical and emotional harassment of Nicole Brown Simpson? The domestic violence issue was a double-edged legal sword. Should those reports be kept from the jury despite the fact that they were accurate? Could they prejudice the jury against the defendant? The issue was not to decide if O. J. was abusive to Nicole. Records indicated that he was. But did the fact that he had been abusive at times mean he was more likely to kill her? It was a complicated legal issue, and Judge Ito gave it a great amount of thought. Ito knew the domestic violence issue was important to the prosecution's case.

A prosecution brief stated, "This is a domestic-violence case involving murder, not a murder case involving domestic violence."[3]

Representing the defense on the issue, Professor Gerald Uelman replied,

> By attaching that label, by saying this case is a domestic violence case, they seek to transform these proceedings from an inquiry into who killed Nicole Brown Simpson and Ronald Goldman on June 12, 1994 into a general inquiry into the character of O. J. Simpson in which he will be called upon to explain every aspect of his life for seventeen years. And there is a fundamental problem with what the prosecution is trying to do here. A defendant must be tried for what he did, not for who he is.[4]

Finally after much deliberation, Judge Lance Ito in a ten-page opinion allowed the prosecution to prove most, but not all, of the domestic violence incidents. Many individuals following the case considered it a domestic violence case involving murder rather than a murder case involving domestic violence. This distinction would appear to make a strong case for the prosecution's ability to establish motive and guilt.

The Media

From the start of the trial, the massive media attention focused on the O. J. Simpson court proceedings had some effect on Judge Lance Ito. Some experts felt he was a bit dazzled by the celebrity aspect of the case. He had met in private with television talk show host Larry King. He also proudly showed off a complimentary note he had received from television celebrity Arsenio Hall.[5]

Television cameras in the courtroom broadcasted every move, facial reaction, and comment. Perhaps the cameras affected not only the judge's behavior, but also the actions of the prosecutors, the defense lawyers, and the witnesses. After all, people tend to act differently when they believe the whole world is watching. The courtroom became, in essence, a stage for a major television event.

The Opening Statement

A prosecution's opening statement told the jury what the evidence would show. Marcia Clark pointed out that in the murder timetable, O. J. Simpson's whereabouts from 9:40 P.M. (when he parted company with Kato Kaelin) until 10:55 P.M. (when limousine driver Allan Park saw him) were unaccounted for. She also touched on blood DNA evidence on which the prosecution had heavily relied. According to tests, the blood drops at the scene matched Simpson's blood and that of only 0.43 percent of the population. In other words, 99.57 percent of the population could be excluded as sources of that blood, but Simpson had to be considered as a source.

Evidence Against O. J. Simpson

Prosecutors painted O. J. Simpson as a raging bull beneath his calm public demeanor. They described him as an obsessed ex-husband.[6]

"Always beneath the surface was this jealousy. There [are] certain things that set him off, that set that fuse burning," said Prosecutor Christopher Darden to the jury.[7] The prosecution alleged that O. J. had physically harassed Nicole on a number of occasions beginning in 1977 when they had first met. The most vivid account occurred on January 1, 1989, and was documented by police records. There were other incidents, including several in 1993. In June 1994, Nicole Brown Simpson contacted the Sojourn Battered Women's Shelter to complain that O. J. Simpson was stalking her. She was afraid and did not know what to do. The contact with Sojourn was just five days prior to the murder.

O. J. Simpson had supposedly made a bizarre and frightening revelation to a former officer of the LAPD named Ron Shipp, after Simpson had returned from Chicago and had been interviewed by detectives. Simpson told Shipp he did not want to take a lie detector test because he had had "dreams" of killing Nicole.[8]

Shipp was a friend of O. J. Simpson's, and his involvement was revealed in the book *Raging Heart* by Sheila Weller, published just months after the murders.

Witnesses

The prosecution's first witness was Sharyn Gilbert, a telephone operator with the 911 emergency service. Gilbert took the 911 call from Nicole Brown Simpson on January 1, 1989. The tape of the call in which Nicole Brown Simpson asked to be protected from O. J. Simpson was played for members of the jury.

The next witness for the prosecution was Detective John

O. J. and Nicole are shown together in happier days.

Edwards of the LAPD. He had been directed to Simpson's mansion to answer the 911 call. When he got there, he found a partially clothed, mud-caked, and battered Nicole Brown Simpson hiding in the bushes. After she opened the gate to the estate, Nicole clung to Detective Edwards and said, "He's going to kill me." (She was referring to O. J. Simpson.) Brown Simpson had a cut on her upper lip. Her forehead was swollen and her eyes blackened. Her cheek was puffy, and she had a hand print on her neck.

Former police officer Ron Shipp was also called to testify. He had known the Simpsons as a couple since before they were married. He had been friends with O. J. Simpson for twenty-six years and was quietly involved with one of their earlier "unofficial" domestic disputes. When Shipp was asked whether he had any opinion about Simpson's guilt or innocence, he replied, "Whoever did this did a heck of a job of framing him."[9]

Denise Brown, Nicole's oldest sister, also testified about O. J. Simpson's explosive temper toward her sister Nicole. Denise Brown's testimony was very emotional. It was difficult to determine the actual effect her testimony had on the jury, however. Denise Brown was the last domestic violence witness in the case against O. J. Simpson.

In His Own Words

At his trial, O. J. Simpson claimed he had never hit Nicole. Letters he had written to her in 1989, presented at trial by the prosecution, seemed to prove otherwise.

Denise Brown, Nicole's oldest sister, is shown here. She testified about O. J. Simpson's explosive temper toward her sister Nicole.

Nicole:

Let me starte [sic] by expressing to you how wrong I was for hurting you. There is no exceptible [sic] excuse for what I did.

Thinking and trying to realize how I got so crazy.

I had such emotional feeling towards you that were as high as any I'd ever felt. It must be because of thosz [sic] feelings that I reacted so emotionally. . . .

With all of that running in me, I just didn't react to [sic] well.[10]

Nicole:

Ever since the other nite [sic] whatever I do keeps turning out wrong. I haven't been able to sleep so I guess it's impaired my judgement.

The detective that spoke to me made it clear I'll have to deal with the law for my action of the other nite [sic] and it's now on my record, so if it ever happens again I would face a matadory [sic] jail term.

We have two healthy great kids. We also have an unlimited future. I only hope I didn't screw it up with this crazy drunken incident. I've never been more disapointed [sic] in myself than I am now. But I know how great our life's [sic] had become leading up to Sat. nite [sic]. And I believe if given the chance this will be our finest year ever.[11]

The Witnesses Continue

Employees of Mezzaluna restaurant and Nicole Brown Simpson's neighbors who heard the dog bark and found the pet were called to testify. They helped to establish a timetable for the crime. The murderer was believed to have been at the scene around 10:15 P.M. or 10:20 P.M. on June 12, 1994.

Police officer Robert Riske was the first officer to arrive

at the scene of the crime. He testified that when he arrived, the only evidence at the murder site was one bloody glove. (This would later be a key point.) Police photos of the scene showed the glove, a dark knit hat, and the envelope containing the sunglasses left at Mezzaluna and later brought to Brown Simpson's home by murder victim Ron Goldman. Other officers involved, including Sergeant David Rossi, and Detectives Ron Phillips and Tom Lange, were also questioned.

One of the most controversial witnesses to appear in the O. J. Simpson trial was Detective Mark Fuhrman of the LAPD. Prosecutor Marcia Clark called Fuhrman to the witness stand and described his prior relationship to the case. In 1985 Mark Fuhrman had responded to a domestic violence call at the Simpsons' home. During an argument, O. J. Simpson had shattered the window of Nicole Brown Simpson's Mercedes-Benz automobile with a baseball bat.

Prejudice?

Prosecutor Clark questioned Fuhrman about racist attitudes he might secretly harbor. In 1984 Fuhrman had confronted an African-American man named Jarvis Bowers for jaywalking. Fuhrman had grabbed Bowers in a chokehold and threatened to kill him. Jarvis Bowers filed an official complaint against Mark Fuhrman.

A woman named Kathleen Bell had also had contact with Mark Fuhrman, in 1985 and 1986. She was a friend of one of Fuhrman's friends. She went public with statements supposedly made by Fuhrman. Bell reported that Fuhrman had said, "when he sees a nigger driving with a white woman he would pull them over."[12]

Bell went on to state that Mark Fuhrman also said "he'd . . . like nothing more than to see all 'niggers' gathered together and killed."[13]

Since Bell had made the statements public in a letter (to the defense team) and on *Larry King Live* on television, Marcia Clark asked Fuhrman (who claimed to have found

Prosecutor Marcia Clark (right) and detective Mark Fuhrman look over Fuhrman's police report from the night of the murders. Fuhrman's testimony proved to be quite controversial.

the bloody glove at the Simpson estate) if he had ever made those statements.

"No I did not," Mark Fuhrman quickly answered.

Other police officers including several African Americans stated they did not believe Fuhrman to be racist. However, Detective Mark Fuhrman's attitude toward minority criminals would come back to haunt him and to play a pivotal role in the case's eventual verdict.

Blood Evidence

The blood evidence in the trial consisted of footprints and DNA results on the blood samples taken from the scene of the crime and from O. J. Simpson's estate. It was determined that rare and expensive Bruno Magli loafers (size 12) had made the bloody footprints at the crime scene. The footprints led away from the bodies of the victims up the front steps and to the rear gate of Nicole Brown Simpson's home. O. J. Simpson (who wears size 12 shoes) claimed he never owned a pair of "ugly" Bruno Magli loafers—but a photo (not available at the time of the trial) later showed Simpson wearing a pair of that type of loafers.

Another blood trail in O. J. Simpson's home led to the foot of his bed. In Simpson's bedroom a pair of bloodstained socks was recovered. DNA tests showed the blood on one spot matched O. J. Simpson's blood type. The blood on another spot matched Nicole Brown Simpson's blood type. DNA tests showed that blood on the door handle of the white Bronco matched O. J. Simpson's blood type. Tests also showed that blood on the center console of the Bronco was consistent with a mixture of O. J. Simpson's blood and the blood of murder victim Ron Goldman. Blood drops to the side of the bloody size 12 footprints left at the murder scene matched O. J. Simpson's blood type. Testimony about the DNA testing was complex and complicated, however, and may have confused and bored members of the jury.

The Knit Cap

Inside the navy blue knit cap found at the crime scene were black hairs from the head of an African-American man. The hairs matched samples taken from the defendant, O. J. Simpson. A head hair found on the shirt of murder victim Ronald Goldman also matched hair samples taken from O. J. Simpson. Carpet fibers were also discovered on the knit cap. The fibers matched the carpet found in the white Ford Bronco owned by O. J. Simpson.

Bloody Gloves

The bloody gloves recovered, one at the murder scene and one at O. J. Simpson's estate, were a pair of uniquely styled Aris Isotoner gloves known as Aris Lights. Aris Lights are a rare model. Richard Rubin, a former executive of Aris Isotoner, was called to view a video of O. J. Simpson at a 1991 Oilers-Bengals NFL playoff game. In the video, Simpson was wearing gloves. When Prosecutor Christopher Darden asked if the gloves were the same type as those found at the murder scene, Rubin replied, "I'm 100 percent certain."[14]

The executive was also positive that O. J. Simpson had

worn the same type of uniquely styled gloves found by the police in earlier television appearances.

The Finger of Guilt Is Pointed

It is the prosecutors who carry the burden of proof in any trial. Under the criminal justice system in the United States, a suspect is always presumed innocent and must be proven to be guilty. Proving a suspect's guilt is a difficult task in a case with no eyewitnesses and no murder weapon. To convict a suspect, jurors must have proof beyond a reasonable doubt of that person's guilt. Marcia Clark, Christopher Darden, and the other prosecutors believed they had presented an excellent case against O. J. Simpson. They had no doubt that he was guilty, but had they done a good job of convincing jurors of Simpson's guilt?

chapter six

THE CASE FOR THE DEFENSE

"Once I decide to take a case I have only one agenda: I want to win. I will try, by every fair and legal means, to get my client off—without regard to the consequences."[1]

—Defense attorney
Alan Dershowitz

After O. J. Simpson and Al Cowlings' futile run from police, attorney Johnnie Cochran spoke with host Bryant Gumbel on *The Today Show*. Said Cochran, "I would urge all your viewers to keep an open mind until you've heard all the evidence, and don't prejudge the case, so that hopefully we can get a fair trial."[2]

The Plan

The prosecution seemed to have a powerful case against O. J. Simpson. Yet public opinion about his guilt or innocence remained split generally along racial lines. The case raised the issue of the past mistakes Los Angeles police had made in dealing with African Americans and other minorities in Los Angeles. But, the prosecution had a mountain of evidence that seemed to point to O. J. Simpson's guilt. The defense set out to prove that mountain of evidence was really just a range of peaks and valleys. Questions about the evidence could create doubt about Simpson's guilt in the minds of the jurors.

Race also became a prime focus for the defense. The defense team wanted to identify the Simpson case as one of a series of many racial abuses by the LAPD. The Los Angeles Police Department was already well known for its part in the Rodney King beating. In that incident, officers had been caught on tape using excessive force and brutal means to restrain King, an African-American suspect.

Opening Statement

"Injustice anywhere is a threat to justice everywhere," said Johnnie Cochran, quoting Dr. Martin Luther King, Jr. in his opening statement.[3] Cochran referred to witnesses Rosa Lopez and Mary Ann Gerchas who could supposedly shed new light on the case. Lopez claimed to have seen Simpson's Bronco parked in the same place throughout the night of the murder. Gerchas claimed to have seen four men leaving Nicole Brown Simpson's house at 10:45 P.M. on the night of the murders. (Later neither witness proved reliable, and, in fact, Mary Ann Gerchas was never called upon to testify.)

The defense's tactic was to plant the seeds of doubt in the jurors' minds. Cochran said Simpson had been framed, set up, and victimized. He claimed he would convince jurors that the evidence was such a mess it would be a crime to convict O. J. Simpson. As the case unfolded, the seeds of doubt planted early in the minds of the jurors began to grow.

O. J. Simpson Defends His Relationship With Nicole

"The media has defined O. J. as this person who was something other than human. But I knew O. J. the friend, I knew O. J. the father," said Joe Bell, a high school teammate of Simpson's in San Francisco. "I've seen the real caring O. J. who would stand for hours taking pictures with people and signing autographs."[4]

Cochran went on to explain how Simpson helped support Nicole Brown Simpson's family and how he made many generous donations to charity. The picture the defense painted of O. J. Simpson differed greatly from the abusive, violent, jealous individual who had been sketched out earlier by the prosecution.

Prosecutors said that O. J. Simpson had stalked his ex-wife. Yet the prosecution presented only one of the several so-called stalking incidents. Two of Nicole's neighbors, a husband and wife, testified to seeing O. J. Simpson walk back and forth for two or three minutes on the sidewalk near Nicole Brown Simpson's home in April 1992 around 11:00 P.M. However, Simpson never stepped onto the property. He only stopped on the sidewalk to look at her house twice before leaving. The couple further testified that they did not even know if Nicole was home at the time.[5]

O. J. Simpson's defense team continued to contradict allegations that Simpson had physically abused Nicole Brown Simpson repeatedly in the past. Photographs of her bruises were explained away in a number of ways. O. J. Simpson suggested that Nicole "picking" at acne on her face caused some of her facial injuries.

The testimony of O. J. Simpson's so-called friend (and former police officer) Ron Shipp was also questioned. The defense vigorously attacked Shipp's motives for testifying, suggesting that he was trying to use Simpson's "friendship" over the years to launch a movie career for himself, trying to capitalize on the publicity of the case.

Discrediting Nicole Brown Simpson

Nicole Brown Simpson's image as a defenseless battered wife and a loving, devoted mother came under fire by the defense. Other aspects of her personality were also questioned. Brown Simpson was presented as a woman living life in the fast lane and enjoying the frequent and sometimes intimate company of various men. The defense wanted to tarnish her image as a saintly mom whose main interest in life was her children. A jury might be less sympathetic to a woman who was not as perfect as she seemed to be. The defense also brought out the idea of other possible motives for her murder.

Faye Resnick Reappears

The relationship between Nicole Brown Simpson and her friend Faye Resnick took a new and bizarre turn when discussed by the defense. Resnick, an admitted drug user, was also a self-confessed confidante of Nicole's. She had heard stories of abuse Nicole had suffered at the hands of O. J. and of threats he had issued.

The defense portrayed Resnick as having a hypnotic control over Brown Simpson. Johnnie Cochran attempted to plant the notion that the presumed "real" killer of Brown Simpson was a deranged member of Faye Resnick's questionable circle of drug friends. Perhaps the killer was a drug dealer owed money by Resnick and the murder was meant to be a message.

When detective Tom Lange was on the witness stand, Cochran asked if he had ever heard of a "Colombian necklace." Lange admitted that the term was known to him.[6]

Cochran went on to explain that a Colombian necklace is a situation where drug dealers slice the neck of a victim in order to scare people and send a message to others who have not paid for their drugs or have been informing to the police. Again, Tom Lange confirmed that drug dealers were known to act in this manner. The implied message of the defense was clear. Nicole Brown Simpson's throat had been slashed. Could the murder have been drug related? Another seed of doubt was planted in the minds of the jurors.

The Furor Over Fuhrman

Use of the very offensive "N-word" and examples of Detective Mark Fuhrman's history of hostility toward African Americans undermined his credibility to the jury. Witnesses stated that Fuhrman had indeed used the N-word on numerous occasions to describe people of color.

Fuhrman had said under oath that he had not used that

word in the past ten years, but he had lied under oath when he insisted he had never used that word.

Mark Fuhrman was also portrayed as a man who had been obsessed with "getting" O. J. Simpson ever since he had answered a domestic violence call at the Simpsons' home in 1985.

The defense claimed O. J. and Nicole as an interracial couple so infuriated Fuhrman that it caused him to target O. J. Simpson at a future date. The defense alleged that when the opportunity presented itself at the scene of the crime in 1994, Detective Mark Fuhrman eagerly leaped at the chance to frame O. J. Simpson for murder by placing the bloody glove there himself.

When an investigator for the defense uncovered audio-tapes of Mark Fuhrman talking about his police work, the defense gained momentum. On the tapes Fuhrman was heard to mutter: "Plant evidence . . . get niggers."[7]

Transcripts of the tapes captured Fuhrman using the crudest racial slurs imaginable and the N-word repeatedly. The defense then began to

Mark Fuhrman claimed under oath that he had never used the N-word. But the defense proved that he lied.

attack Mark Fuhrman with furor. "This man is an unspeakable disgrace," proclaimed Johnnie Cochran. "He's been unmasked to the whole world for what he is." Cochran went on to say, "Mark Fuhrman is a lying, perjuring, genocidal racist and from that point [1985] on, any time he could get O. J. Simpson he would!"[8]

The defense contended that Fuhrman had picked up a bloody glove at the murder scene, secretly transported it to the Simpson estate, and placed the glove outside Simpson's home in an attempt to frame Simpson for murder. Fuhrman later used his Fifth Amendment right not to speak rather than submit to further cross-examination.

A Bloody Mistake

Forensic evidence compiled in the O. J. Simpson case was supervised by criminologist Dennis Fung. Under questioning by defense lawyer Barry Scheck, it was revealed that Andrea Mazzola had assisted Fung in processing the evidence at the crime scene and at O. J. Simpson's estate. It was only Mazzola's third time at a crime scene, and her inexperience proved to be a vulnerable target. Mazzola had collected important evidence. Never before, however, had Mazzola had the primary responsibility for collecting blood evidence from a crime scene. The possibility that she might have made a mistake always existed.

In fact, investigators had made a number of crucial mistakes, and the defense team was aware of those mistakes.

Detective Phil Vannatter had carried around O. J. Simpson's blood sample in a vial in an unsealed envelope for three hours before booking it. The defense argued that 1.5 cc's of Simpson's blood could not be accounted for by the prosecution, thus planting the idea that perhaps it had been "placed" at the crime scene in order to frame Simpson.

The criminologists failed to find O. J. Simpson's blood on the back gate or on Simpson's socks during the original investigation. It was only found several weeks after Simpson's blood sample had been taken and carried around by Vannatter. The suggestion was planted that blood from Simpson's sample given at police headquarters could have been used to plant evidence at the scenes in order to frame Simpson.

Furthermore, the criminologists did not count the blood samples (at the scene) when they collected them, did not count the blood samples when they were put in tubes for drying, and did not count them when they were taken out of the tubes. No documented booking of samples occurred until June 16. Again, the defense implied that perhaps the police had "planted" some of the blood found at the scene.

Contaminated Evidence

The hair samples found at the murder scene were also challenged by the defense as shoddy investigative work by the police. The defense revealed that the police had contaminated the crime scene by covering the bodies with a blanket from Nicole Brown Simpson's home. O. J. Simpson had visited before. The fibers found could have been there from previous visits. If a clean sheet provided by the police had been used, the evidence would not have been tainted.

Use of that blanket cast doubt on all hair and fiber samples that were collected from the victims' bodies.

It was also revealed that the bodies of the victims were dragged around the crime scene *before* hair and fiber samples were taken from their clothing. That was proof of possible further evidence contamination.

The Cap and Gloves

Defense attorney Johnnie Cochran put on a knit cap in court in an attempt to disprove the prosecution's theory that O. J. Simpson wore a cap the night of the crime to disguise his identity. The demonstration seemed to impress the jury. A knit cap certainly did not disguise the identity of Cochran. Of course, Cochran was in a well-lit courtroom, not a dark alley, and he was not wearing nondescript dark clothing.

The bloody gloves were even more important pieces of evidence. The prosecutors had shown photos of O. J. Simpson wearing gloves just like the ones found at the murder scene. The defense team wanted to prove that O. J. Simpson could not have worn the gloves found at the scene. It wanted Simpson to try on the gloves that were found. "If it doesn't fit, you must acquit!" stated defense attorney Johnnie Cochran, speaking of one of the gloves found at the murder scene.

The prosecution did not want Simpson to try on the actual gloves. It claimed it did not want the evidence contaminated. Or, perhaps it realized that the bloody gloves might have shrunk once the blood dried and would no longer fit properly, even if they had once belonged to Simpson.

They wanted Simpson to try on new gloves that were exact duplicates of the murder-scene gloves. The defense wanted to use the gloves found at the scene.

Judge Ito ruled that O. J. Simpson would wear thin sanitary (rubber) gloves before trying on the bloody gloves. When O. J. Simpson tried on the murder gloves, the fit appeared too small and too tight. The prosecutors contended that the fit was the way Simpson wore all of his gloves and that the sanitary gloves also added to the distortion of the fit. The doubts that had been raised by the defense began to gather momentum in the minds of some.

More Mistakes

The defense continued to expose improper techniques that had been used by the police to gather evidence against O. J. Simpson. They had failed to obtain a warrant to enter Simpson's residence and instead came up with a story about wanting desperately to notify Simpson of what had happened. This raised questions about a possible frame-up plan by the police.

Furthermore, the police misstated facts on the search warrant, causing Judge Lance Ito eventually to find that Detective Philip Vannatter was "at least reckless" in regard to the truth.[9] The police also failed to notify the coroner's office in a timely fashion as required by LAPD procedures.

Stop the Cover-Up!

Lead defense attorney Johnnie Cochran urged jurors in the O. J. Simpson murder trial to, "Stop this cover-up." Defense attorney Barry Scheck told the jurors they could not trust any of the DNA analysis of the blood because of police contamination and tampering. Said Scheck, "If the messenger can't be believed, why should the message be?"[10]

The team for the defense urged jurors to search their hearts and minds and to make a stand against corruption in the criminal justice system by rejecting the police evidence and by finding O. J. Simpson not guilty of all charges.

"That's what I'm asking you to do," said Johnnie Cochran. "Stop this cover-up. Stop this cover-up. If you don't stop it then who? Do you think the police department

O. J. Simpson demonstrates the fit of the bloody gloves he was asked to try on during the trial.

is going to stop it? Do you think the D.A.'s office is going to stop it? Do you think we can stop it by ourselves? It has to be stopped by you!"[11]

It was clear that the defense had turned the tables in the trial. The defense team made it seem as if the LAPD were on trial. It had also raised doubts in a number of key areas in the prosecution's case. Would the jury trust the evidence the prosecution had presented?

To Tell the Truth

The following excerpt of a Nancy Snyderman interview with Alan Dershowitz on *Good Morning America* in the middle of the O. J. Simpson trial talked about police perjury—lying under oath in court. Perhaps, Dershowitz seemed to suggest, the police were "out to get" O. J. Simpson and did what was needed to make a case.

Nancy Snyderman: Mark Fuhrman did hold up yesterday. Were you surprised?

Alan Dershowitz: No. That's what they are trained to do. Police are trained to be cool. They're professional witnesses. The Mollen Commission in New York after reviewing thousands of hours of police testimony said, police perjury is rampant in the courts, but lawyers can't get at the perjury unless they can confront the witnesses with their own words. And the irony here. . . .

Nancy Snyderman: You're telling me that police departments tell their detectives that it's okay to lie?

Alan Dershowitz: Not only do police departments tell their detectives it's okay to lie, they learn it at the academy. They have a word for it. It's called, 'testilying.' And they do it coolly and they do it in a way that they can't be broken down unless you can confront them with their own words.[12]

The defense had established the fact that Fuhrman had lied about using the N-word. Perhaps he had also lied about other things.

The Prosecution's Plea

Prosecutor Christopher Darden reminded the jury that the tensions that led up to the murders started building long before the crimes were committed on June 12, 1994. He stated that Nicole Brown Simpson had been worn down by her ex-husband's relentless persistence.

O. J. Simpson Speaks

Despite protests from prosecutor Marcia Clark, Judge Lance Ito allowed O. J. Simpson to make his longest formal statement since pleading not guilty. Simpson was never called upon to testify in his own defense. Prosecutor Clark objected to Simpson's speaking after the prosecution and defense had both rested their cases, but Judge Ito never explicitly ruled on Clark's objection. Simpson made his statement before he formally waived his right to testify on Friday, September 22, 1995.

In his only personal response to the court case, O. J. Simpson had this to say:

Good morning, your honor. As much as I would like to address some of the misrepresentations made about myself and my Nicole concerning our life together, I am mindful of the mood and stamina of this jury.

I have confidence, a lot more, it seems, than Miss Clark has, of their integrity and that they will find as the record stands now that I did not, could not and would not have committed this crime. I have four kids. Two kids I haven't seen in a year. They ask me every week, "Dad, how much longer . . . before this trial is over?"

Judge Ito started to interrupt so Simpson hurriedly finished: "I want this trial over, over."

The judge then cut him off. Said Judge Ito, "Mr. Simpson you do understand your right to testify as a witness and you chose to rest your case at this. . . ."

Simpson nodded and Ito said, "All right. Thank you very much sir."[13]

Closing Arguments

Marcia Clark for the Prosecution.

It would be completely understandable if you [the members of the jury] were to feel angry and disgusted with Mark Fuhrman. As we all are. . . . Did he lie when he testified here in this courtroom saying that he did not use racial epithets in the last ten years? Yes! Is he a racist? Yes! Is he the worst the LAPD. has to offer? Yes.

But the fact that Mark Fuhrman is a racist and lied about it on the witness stand does not mean that we haven't proven the defendant guilty beyond a reasonable doubt.[14]

Clark concluded that the prosecution had proved opportunity, identity, and motive. O. J. Simpson could not document his whereabouts for the crucial period of time when Nicole Brown Simpson and Ron Goldman were murdered. Simpson was identified as the man whose blood was at the murder scene. The motive (which the prosecution is not required to prove) was sexual rage. Mr. Simpson had terrorized his wife for years.

Johnnie Cochran for the Defense.

> Your verdict goes far beyond the walls of this courtroom. Your verdict talks about justice in America and it talks about the police and whether they should be above the law. . . . Maybe that's why you were selected. . . . Maybe there's someone in your background . . . that helps you understand that this is wrong. . . . Maybe you're the right people, at the right time, at the right place to say, no more—we're not going to have this.[15]

Christopher Darden for the Prosecution.

> You can't send a message to Fuhrman, you can't send a message to the LAPD, you can't eradicate racism within the LAPD or within the L.A. community or within the nation as a whole by delivering a verdict of not guilty, in a case like this. The evidence is there. You just have to find your way through the smoke.[16]

chapter seven

THE JURY DECIDES

THE VERDICT—The O. J. Simpson murder trial (which some legal experts dubbed "The Trial of the Century") was a long, drawn-out affair that lasted more than eight months. It was a trial involving lying witnesses, instant celebrity status for the participants, complex and at times boring and confusing scientific evidence, explosive clashes of strong personalities, racism, prejudice, intricate legal strategies, and massive media coverage. The trial dominated the lives of many Americans as they watched on television and read the news about the real-life drama unfolding each day in a California courtroom.

Names like Marcia Clark, Johnnie Cochran, Chris Darden, Kato Kaelin, Allan Park, Fred Goldman, Lance Ito, Faye Resnick, and others became the source of countless conversations about the American judicial system. And, of course, the name of Detective Mark Fuhrman became an infamous symbol of racism and prejudice in police work.

There were so many people and issues involved in the case that many Americans lost track of what was going on at some points during the eight-month legal marathon. Some people watched, read about, or heard only parts of the evidence presented by both sides and formulated an opinion based on that limited knowledge.

However, most people seemed to have a definite opinion. There were few middle-of-the-road opinions about the trial. Most black Americans favored an innocent verdict while most white Americans favored a guilty verdict.

The Jury

Sometimes, public opinion about a court case can differ greatly from the opinions formed by jurors. The jury in the O. J. Simpson case was not subjected to the same television shows and news stories that the general public saw. The jury was concerned only with the facts that had been presented in court by the prosecution and the defense.

Judge Lance Ito made every attempt to keep the sequestered jury from hearing and seeing outside reports that might have ultimately influenced or swayed their opinions regarding O. J. Simpson's guilt or innocence.

During the early parts of the trial, one juror was discharged after she admitted to watching videotaped episodes of *Beverly Hills 90210* and *Melrose Place* with all of the commercials deleted from the tapes.[1] Another juror was discharged because he had watched cartoons on television with his grandson. During the eight months of the O. J. Simpson trial, ten of the original twelve jurors were replaced by alternates.

A Foreperson Is Chosen

After the prosecution and defense rested their cases, a foreperson, a leader, was picked to guide the jury through deliberations. Amanda Cooley, an African-American woman, was selected. Cooley was one of the best-educated members of the jury, with several years of college to her credit. Jury deliberations were set to begin on October 2, 1995.

The Verdict

On October 2, 1995, the attorneys were notified that the jury had reached a verdict after asking for a read-back of limo driver Allan Park's testimony. It was the only testimony the jury wanted to go over. The jury's decision was quick and without hesitation, much to the surprise of most people following the case.

It took the jury only some four hours to reach a verdict in a complex case that had taken almost a year to present. Judge Lance Ito ruled that the verdict would be announced on the following morning.

On the morning of October 3, 1995, Judge Ito's courtroom was tense with anticipation.

"Madam Foreperson," Judge Ito said, "would you please open the envelope and check the condition of the verdict forms?" The foreperson checked the ballots.

"Are they the same forms you signed and are they in order?" Ito questioned.

"Yes they are," replied Cooley.

Judge Ito looked to the defendant. "Mr. Simpson, would you please stand and face the jury?" As O. J. Simpson rose, a court deputy delivered the verdict envelope to the judge's court clerk. The clerk slowly read the verdict.

"We the jury in the above-entitled action, find the defendant Orenthal James Simpson not guilty of the crime of murder in violation of Penal Code Section 187A, a felony, upon Nicole Brown Simpson, a human being, as charged in Count One of the information."

A Free Man

The clerk read the second verdict in the murder of Ronald Goldman. It too was "not guilty." As the defense team celebrated, the prosecutors sat in stunned silence.

"The defendant, having been acquitted of both charges," Judge Lance Ito began, "is ordered released forthwith. All right. We stand on recess."

The jurors began to file out; their duty done. Kim Goldman, murder victim Ron Goldman's sister, sobbed. Fred Goldman, Ron's father, turned toward the acquitted O. J. Simpson and muttered his personal opinion of the verdict.

Undaunted, a happy and vindicated O. J. Simpson left the courtroom. As he returned by van to his estate, he rode past cheering fans that supported the "not guilty" verdict.

Many people in the white community were convinced of

O. J. Simpson's guilt and were totally stunned by the verdict. But, there were reasons why the jury voted the way it did.

Inside the Jury

It was later learned that the first vote of the jury was ten for acquittal and two for conviction. After that initial vote, the jurors raised some of the following issues for review.

If Ron Goldman had bruises on his knuckles from fighting back during the murder, why didn't O. J. Simpson have any bruises on his body?

If the bloody glove had been pulled off of Simpson's hand during the fight, why wasn't it inside out?

Kim Goldman (victim Ron Goldman's sister) and Fred Goldman (Ron's father) were visibly unhappy with the criminal jury's decision to acquit O. J. Simpson of both murder charges.

The fact that the bloody gloves did not seem to fit O. J. Simpson was also a key factor in the jury's decision.

Limo driver Allan Park's timetable about the events at O. J. Simpson's estate seemed confusing. Park had claimed Simpson's Bronco was not parked at the Rockingham Estate when he had first arrived, but it was there by the time they (he and Simpson) left for the airport. The jury reviewed Mr. Park's testimony and did not find it foolproof enough.

The jury had reasonable doubt concerning O. J. Simpson's guilt. Thus, the acquittal.

Time Stands Still

For a few moments on the morning of October 2, 1995, time seemed to stand still as Americans gathered around television sets to listen to the O. J. Simpson verdict.

Following the verdict, many polls conducted by newspapers and radio stations indicated that some in the general public felt that justice had not been served and that a guilty man had been freed. In one *USA Today* Gallup Poll, 56 percent of the people interviewed (more than half) did not agree with the verdict. Thirty-three percent of those interviewed agreed with the verdict, while 11 percent were undecided.[2]

The criminal case against O. J. Simpson was officially over, but the controversy surrounding the murders and the verdict had not yet been laid to rest.

chapter eight

WAS JUSTICE SERVED?

REACTIONS—There were decidedly mixed reactions to the verdict. Some felt O. J. Simpson had been rightfully vindicated. Others felt Simpson had gotten away with murder. Still others blamed the verdict on the prejudices of the LAPD and the overconfident arrogance of the prosecuting team. There was another faction that claimed wealth and fame could always "buy" justice—even in a murder trial.

There was also a question on people's minds after the not guilty verdict was reached. If O. J. Simpson did not commit the murders, who did and why? The Los Angeles police decided not to investigate further. They felt they had found the killer in O. J. Simpson and had presented a strong case to prove his guilt. There would be no further action in the criminal case.

There would, however, be civil action filed against O. J. Simpson by the families of Ron Goldman and Nicole Simpson Brown. In a civil lawsuit, a person cannot be punished with time in jail, but he or she can be held responsible for infringing on the victim's civil rights. If O. J. Simpson were found guilty of violating the victims' civil rights, he would have to pay the victims' families.

The Issue of Domestic Violence Lives On

Activists fighting domestic violence felt the Simpson verdict provoked more incidents of abuse. They believed abusive husbands read the verdict as a possible means of escaping legal prosecution.[1]

Less than two weeks after O. J. Simpson was acquitted, a husband in Northern California slashed his wife's face and neck with a butcher knife. As the assault was in progress the man told his wife, "I will kill you. O. J. got away with it and so will I."[2] The wife survived the assault and reported the incident and her husband's words to police. He did not escape punishment for his deed, but the man's mindset was cause for alarm. In fact, after the verdict, women who felt they would not get help stopped calling domestic violence hotlines in some states.

Gail Pincus of the Domestic Abuse Center in Los Angeles summed up the feelings of some of her clients after the Simpson case concluded. "To the women [the verdict] said, it doesn't matter who you tell, what you do, because if he wants to kill you, he can get away with it."[3] Meanwhile, supporters of O. J. Simpson were proclaiming that American justice for African Americans had truly been served.

Was the verdict in the O. J. Simpson case a glorious victory or a stunning defeat for the American justice system? Those who felt that justice had not been served pointed fingers at the media circus that surrounded the proceedings. Judge Ito's fascination with celebrities was also a target for those who were unhappy with the verdict. And, of course, there was the prejudice of Detective Mark Fuhrman.

"If Mark Fuhrman had done his job right, things might have turned out differently," said Police Sergeant Craig Novick of New Jersey. "A lot of officers thought that his conduct was completely unprofessional."[4]

Those who thought the verdict was a glorious victory found new faith in the American justice system.

O. J. Simpson's Image

"Was O. J. Simpson really innocent?" This was a question Simpson would have to live with from then on. Celebrities rely on an adoring public in order to make a living. Simpson had to win back the trust of the public in order to get on with his life in the public eye. People wanted to know what plans he had for the future. What were his innermost feelings about the murders? To answer his public, O. J. Simpson scheduled a television interview with hosts Tom Brokaw and Katie Couric on *Dateline NBC*. The live event was to be broadcast on October 11, 1995.

Only hours before what was expected to be one of the most widely watched television events in history, O. J. Simpson, on the advice of his lawyers, decided not to appear on *Dateline NBC*. In an earlier conversation with NBC news president Andrew Lack, Simpson had agreed to answer questions with no restrictions.

When Simpson's lawyers learned of the conditions of the interview, they weighed the possible negative consequences against the possible positive results of such an interview and saw no balance between them. In a statement read by attorney Johnnie Cochran, O. J. Simpson said:

> It was agreed that this would be a conversation not a confrontation . . . however, it has become clear that NBC had, perhaps in an attempt to appease diverse public viewpoints, concluded that this would be a time and an opportunity to retry me.[5]

Some analysts viewed Simpson's refusal to appear in a more condemning fashion. "It's a pretty succinct way of saying I did it," concluded Mandy Grunwald, a political consultant. "They [Simpson's attorneys] are smart enough to know that his pulling out will be perceived as admitting guilt. If they fear that less than what he might say on the air, that's pretty striking."[6]

chapter nine

O. J. SIMPSON IS BACK IN COURT

IN THE COURTROOM— O. J. Simpson was brought back to court for a civil trial filed by the families of victims Ron Goldman and Nicole Brown Simpson. A civil action is brought to recover some civil right or to obtain compensation for some wrong that is not considered a crime. A criminal conviction can result in punishment (such as jail time). A civil conviction can result in compensation, in this case, money paid to the victims' families.

The plaintiffs felt that Simpson was responsible for the deaths of Ron Goldman and Nicole Brown Simpson and therefore he owed punitive damages (money) to their families to compensate them for their losses.

The civil case was tried in Santa Monica, California. It raised many of the same issues that had been debated during the criminal trial. However, at stake, based on the outcome of the trial, was O. J. Simpson's money, not his personal freedom.

New Lawyers

In the civil trial the Dream

Team defense would not be in control of reestablishing O. J. Simpson's innocence. (Criminal lawyers are not necessarily skilled in civil law.) This time, leading the defense was attorney Robert Baker. The families of Ron Goldman and Nicole Brown Simpson had Daniel Petrocelli representing them.

A Different Format

The standard of proof required in a civil case is much lower than that required in a criminal case. Jurors in a civil case are asked to make their ultimate decision based on a "preponderance of evidence."

A preponderance of evidence means a decision in favor of the plaintiffs can be reached if the jury determines there is more than a 50 percent possibility the defendant is guilty.

O. J. Simpson could be held financially responsible for the deaths of Ron and Nicole Brown Simpson if the jury could be convinced that there was more than a 50 percent probability that Simpson was responsible for the slayings. In a civil case, the "reasonable doubt" defense does not come into play. In addition, in a civil trial only nine of the twelve jurors need to agree for a verdict to be reached.

Wrongful Death Suit

O. J. Simpson was brought to trial in the civil case in what is known as a wrongful-death suit. Most wrongful-death suits involve car crashes, plane wrecks, and medical malpractice instances, where wealthy car companies, airlines, doctors, and hospitals can be put on trial.

It is very unusual to have a wrongful-death suit in the case of a homicide. In most cases, defendants in murder cases do not have financial resources worth pursuing. In the case of O. J. Simpson, the wealthy celebrity, that was not so.

The Jury in the Civil Trial

The racial makeup of the jury for the O. J. Simpson civil trial consisted of nine whites, one Hispanic, one Asian, and one person of black and Hispanic ancestry—quite different than the mostly black jury that had decided the criminal case.

Superior Court Judge Hiroshi Fujisaki presided over the civil trial of O. J. Simpson. This trial did not receive the massive media attention of the criminal proceedings. It was not televised. Judge Fujisaki also banned photographers from the courtroom. He ordered the lawyers and witnesses involved not to discuss the case with the media.

The Case *Against* O. J. Simpson

Attorney Daniel Petrocelli portrayed O. J. Simpson to the jury as an egomaniac obsessed with his ex-wife, whom he routinely abused. Petrocelli stated that when Simpson was unable to keep his wife from ending their stormy relationship, he brutally killed her. The plaintiffs' attorney backed up his arguments by reviewing evidence (used in the criminal case) that he said linked Simpson to the crime. Once again, Ron Goldman was portrayed as an innocent bystander, doing a favor for a friend, who ended up in the wrong place at the wrong time.

Some new evidence was allowed in the civil trial. The testimony from the operator of a battered women's hotline that a woman named Nicole called to say she had been and was being stalked by her famous husband was newly introduced. Testimony also showed that O. J. Simpson had failed a lie detector test following the murders.

O. J. Simpson is seen leaving the courtroom after the first day of the civil trial.

The testimony of former detective Mark Fuhrman was excluded from the civil case.

The Case *for* O. J. Simpson

Defense attorneys Robert Baker and Robert Blasier accused the plaintiffs of "character assassination" against O. J. Simpson. Baker also blasted the evidence against Simpson as "garbage."

"Evidence gathered by the LAPD was corrupted, contaminated, tampered with or planted," defense attorney Blasier told the jury. "You cannot rely on physical evidence. What was picked up off the ground was not necessarily the same as went to the lab."[1]

A New Verdict

The mostly white jury hearing the evidence presented in the O. J. Simpson wrongful-death suit found O. J. Simpson liable for the deaths of Nicole Brown Simpson and Ron Goldman. As mentioned previously, a jury in a civil trial does not have to consider reasonable doubt. In fact, few people (especially legal experts) were surprised by the decision.

Compensatory Damages

A judgment of $8.5 million was leveled against O. J. Simpson in the wrongful-death civil trial. The money represented funeral costs for Ron Goldman and the loss of his companionship for his family. Nicole Brown Simpson's family did not seek compensatory damages from O. J. Simpson.

Punitive Damages

In a wrongful-death suit a jury can also award the plaintiffs financial damages known as punitive damages. In the civil case against O. J. Simpson, the jury ordered that Simpson also pay $25 million in punitive damages to the relatives of Nicole Brown Simpson and Ronald Goldman.

"We came to the conclusion that Mr. Simpson should not profit from these murders," said juror Stephen Strati in explaining how the panel arrived at the huge sum awarded to the plaintiffs.[2]

What the Public Had to Say

- "Was justice done? No. If he's guilty he should be guilty on both. He wasn't proven innocent—he was proven not guilty."[3] —a middle-aged white female

- "I really think they're robbing him. I don't think he did it. I don't think he should have to pay them anything."[4] —a young black female

- "I'm glad it's over. Now we can get on to more important things."[5] —a middle-aged white male

chapter ten

A STAR FALLS FROM GRACE

SECOND VERDICT—A jury made up of mostly minorities found O. J. Simpson not guilty of murder in a criminal case. A jury of almost all whites found O. J. Simpson liable in the wrongful deaths of Nicole Brown Simpson and Ron Goldman in a civil case based mainly on the same facts. The two cases served to heighten America's awareness of two of its most troubling issues—domestic violence and racism.

"There is a difference in how people perceive facts based on their background and experience," said Charles Jones, a Rutgers University criminal law professor, at the conclusion of the civil case.[1]

Many people thought the racial makeup of the two juries made the difference in their ultimate decisions. However, in reality, the juries reached different decisions based on different standards of evaluation. That is not to say that the racial makeup of each jury may not have played a role in how it viewed the same evidence. No one, not even legal experts, can be certain of the effect of race on the verdict. Some white people claimed the second verdict rebalanced the scales of justice. Some black commentators claimed it was evidence of still more discrimination. Perhaps each jury saw the same evidence in a different way. Regardless, the O. J. Simpson trial stands as one of the most controversial court cases in history.

Fame by Association

The O. J. Simpson trial made short-term celebrities of numerous individuals involved in the case. Members of both the prosecuting and defense teams wrote books. Witnesses wrote books. Friends wrote books. Even O. J. Simpson wrote a book.

Johnnie Cochran and Marcia Clark became television celebrities. Detective Mark Fuhrman retired from the LAPD and moved to another state. As for O. J. Simpson, the fame he had acquired as a star athlete and Hollywood celebrity turned to infamy.

"He will be the Frankenstein of celebrities, but he will be a celebrity and people will pay to see him," predicted Howard J. Rubenstein, the head of a New York public relations firm, after the amount of the damages had been disclosed. "Being a celebrity in America does not mean being applauded, it means being a curiosity."[2]

Faded Glory

In the years after the trial, O. J. Simpson generally stayed out of the public eye. He quietly became a topic of yesterday's conversations, occasionally making the news for participating in a celebrity golf tournament. The O. J. Simpson murder trial became a scarred wound that healed, but it remains a sore point in legal history. At its height, the case divided America along racial lines. Even today, when the case is mentioned, there is rarely a lukewarm response to the trial's verdict. Did O. J. Simpson get away with murder or was he correctly judged not guilty? What do you think?

Questions for Discussion

1. In your opinion, is O. J. Simpson guilty or innocent? Explain your answer.

2. Did race play a role in the different decisions of the criminal and civil juries? Explain your answer.

3. Did publicity and media attention affect the court proceedings? Explain your answer.

4. Should a defense attorney fight for absolute truth or the rights of his or her client if those two things are in conflict? Explain your answer.

5. Does money or wealth play a key role in how justice is dispensed in America? Explain your answer.

6. Would the outcome of the trial have differed if the defendant were not a famous celebrity? Explain your answer.

7. Was the civil trial of O. J. Simpson fair and just? Explain your answer.

8. Should circumstantial evidence be enough to convict a defendant in a murder trial? Explain your answer.

9. Why did O. J. Simpson not take the stand to testify in his own defense? Explain your answer.

10. Did the police violate O. J. Simpson's civil rights at any time during their investigation? Explain your answer.

11. Should O. J. Simpson's history of domestic violence have been part of the criminal case? Explain your answer.

12. Is it is possible for a criminal to get away with murder in America? Explain your answer.

Chronology

1977—Nicole Brown and O. J. Simpson begin to date.

1985—Nicole Brown and O. J. Simpson marry.

1988—O. J. Simpson becomes enraged after his sister-in-law (Denise Brown) tells him he takes Nicole for granted.

1988 or 1989—O. J. Simpson strikes Nicole in the face while in the back seat of a limo.

January 1989—Police come to the Simpson home after Nicole Brown Simpson places a 911 call for help. She tells police that O. J. Simpson has beaten her.

1989—O. J. Simpson pleads no contest to spousal battery.

January 1992—Nicole Brown Simpson moves out of the home she shared with O. J. into her own home.

February 1992—Nicole Brown Simpson files for divorce. O. J. Simpson starts to stalk his former wife.

April 1992—O. J. Simpson spies on his wife while she is in her home with another man.

October 1992—The divorce between O. J. Simpson and Nicole Brown Simpson is final.

October 1993—O. J. Simpson enters Nicole Brown Simpson's home and threatens her verbally leading to another 911 call.

January 1994—Nicole Brown Simpson moves to a new home.

May 1994—Nicole Brown Simpson celebrates her birthday. She gives a birthday gift from O. J. Simpson back to him.

June 12, 1994—Sydney Simpson has a dance recital at her school. Nicole Brown Simpson and Ron Goldman are murdered that same night.

Chapter Notes

Chapter 1. A Date With Death

1. CNN Online, O. J. Simpson Trial News: "The Murder" September 25, 1994, <http://www.cnn.com/US/OJ/murder/index.html> (October 3, 2000).

2. Official records of the Los Angeles Police Department, 911 tape of call from Nicole Brown Simpson, October 25, 1993.

3. Associated Press, "O. J. the Celebrity Hero Becomes a Defendant," *The Courier News* (Bridgewater, N.J.), September 25, 1994, p. A4.

Chapter 2. A Famous Suspect

1. Helen Benedict, *Virgin or Vamp: How the Press Covers Sex Crimes* (New York: Oxford University Press, 1992), p. 7.

2. Vincent Bugliosi, *Outrage: The Five Reasons O. J. Simpson Got Away With Murder* (New York: W. W. Norton and Company, 1996), p. 270.

3. Ibid.

4. The Associated Press, "O. J. the Celebrity Hero Becomes a Defendant," *The Courier News* (Bridgewater, N.J.), September 25, 1994, p. A4.

5. Ralph Hickok, *Who's Who of Sports Champions* (Boston: Houghton Mifflin, 1995), p. 727.

6. Christopher Darden With Jess Walter, *In Contempt* (New York: Harper Collins, 1996), p. 76.

7. Associated Press, "O. J. the Celebrity Becomes a Defendant," p. A4.

8. Ibid.

9. Darden, p. 84.

10. Los Angeles Police Department's Interrogation of O. J. Simpson transcribed from tape, June 13, 1994.

11. Interview in the *San Francisco Chronicle* Datebook, April 1974. Reprinted by the Associated Press "O. J. the Celebrity Hero Becomes a Defendant," p. A4.

Chapter 3. O. J. Simpson Accused and Pursued

1. LAPD's Interrogation of O. J. Simpson, transcribed from tape June 13, 1994.

2. Ibid.

3. Ibid.

4. Ibid.

5. CNN Online O. J. Simpson Trial News: "The Arrest," June 14, 1994, <http://www.cnn.com/US/OJ/arrest/ index.html> (April 1, 1999).

6. Ibid.

7. Jeffrey Toobin, *The Run of His Life: The People vs. O. J. Simpson* (New York: Random House, 1996), pp. 97–98, 101.

8. Vincent Bugliosi, *Outrage: The Five Reasons O. J. Simpson Got Away With Murder* (New York: W. W. Norton & Co., 1996), p. 100.

Chapter 4. The Criminal Trial Begins

1. Christopher Darden With Jess Walter, *In Contempt* (New York: Harper Collins, 1996), p. 117.

2. Ibid.

Chapter 5. The Case for the Prosecution

1. Marcia Clark With Teresa Carpenter, *Without a Doubt* (New York: Viking Penguin, 1997), p. 3.

2. Christopher Darden With Jess Walter, *In Contempt* (New York: Harper Collins, 1996), p. 124.

3. Jeffrey Toobin, *The Run of His Life: The People vs. O. J. Simpson* (New York: Random House, 1996), p. 237.

4. Ibid.

5. Ibid., p. 232.

6. Associated Press, "O. J. Was Raging Bull, Jury Told," *The Courier News* (Bridgewater, N.J.), September 28, 1995, p. A3.

7. Ibid.

8. Toobin, p. 265.

9. Clark, p. 285.

10. Darden, p. 280

11. Ibid.

12. Toobin, p. 315.

13. Ibid.

14. Associated Press, "Expert Links O. J. to Gloves," *The Courier News* (Bridgewater, N.J.), September 13, 1995, p. A3.

Chapter 6. The Case for the Defense

1. Alan Dershowitz, *Reasonable Doubts* (New York: Simon & Schuster, 1996), p. 87.

2. Jeffrey Toobin, *The Run of His Life: The People vs. O. J. Simpson* (New York: Random House, 1996), p. 171.

3. Associated Press, "Somber Prosecution Team Absorbs Stunning Loss," *The Courier News* (Bridgewater, N.J.), October 4, 1995, p. A7.

4. Associated Press, "O. J. the Celebrity Hero Becomes a Defendant," *The Courier News* (Bridgewater, N.J.), September 25, 1994, p. A3.

5. Vincent Bugliosi, *Outrage: The Five Reasons O. J. Simpson Got Away With Murder* (New York: W. W. Norton & Co., 1996), p. 137.

6. Marcia Clark With Teresa Carpenter, *Without a Doubt* (New York: Viking Penguin, 1997), p. 308.

7. Associated Press, "A Look Back at the Trial of the Century," *The Courier News* (Bridgewater, N.J.), October 4, 1995, p. A6.

8. Associated Press, "Cochran Pushes for an Acquittal," *The Courier News* (Bridgewater, N.J.), September 29, 1995, p. A3.

9. Dershowitz, p. 31.

10. Newsday, "The Defense Rests," *The Courier News* (Bridgewater, N.J.), September 29, 1995, p. A3.

11. Ibid.

12. Dershowitz, p. 60.

13. Associated Press, "TV Viewers Miss O. J. Waive Rights," *The Courier News* (Bridgewater, N.J.), September 23, 1995, p. A3.

14. Clark, p. 462.

15. Bugliosi, p. 199.

16. Ibid.

Chapter 7. The Jury Decides

1. Jeffrey Toobin, *The Run of His Life: The People vs. O. J. Simpson* (New York: Random House, 1996), p. 206.

2. The Los Angeles Times, "Not Guilty!" *The Courier News* (Bridgewater, N.J.), October 4, 1995, p. 1.

Chapter 8. Was Justice Served?

1. Associated Press, "O. J. Verdict Spurs Fear for Battered," *The Courier News* (Bridgewater, N.J.), October 22, 1995, p. A6.

2. Ibid.

3. Ibid.

4. Paul H. B. Shin, "Central Jersey Pauses for O. J.," *The Courier News* (Bridgewater, N.J.), October 4, 1995, p. A9.

5. The Washington Post, "O. J. Backs Out," *The Courier News* (Bridgewater, N.J.) October 12, 1995, p. 1.

6. Ibid.

Chapter 9. O. J. Simpson Is Back in Court

1. "The Simpson Case," February 4, 1997, <http://www.cgi.cnn.com/us/9702/04/simpson.verdicts/> (April 1, 1999).

2. Combined Wire Services, "O. J. Hit for $25M," *The Courier News* (Bridgewater, N.J.), February 5, 1997, p. A4.

3. "Local Reaction to the Simpson Verdict," (Bridgewater, N.J.), February 11, 1997, p. A4.

4. Wil S. Shamlin and Vincent Paterno, "Simpson Saga Was Getting Old," *The Courier News* (Bridgewater, N.J.), February 11, 1997, p. A1.

5. "Local Reaction to the Simpson Verdict," p. A4.

Chapter 10. A Star Falls From Grace

1. Combined Wire Services, "O. J. Won't Go Broke," *The Courier News* (Bridgewater, N.J.), February 6, 1997, p. A1.

2. Ibid.

Glossary

arraignment—The process in which a person accused of a crime is called to court to answer the changes against him or her.

brief—The facts of a case that are prepared in written or oral form by an attorney.

circumstantial evidence—Evidence that seems to point to a conclusion but is not concrete.

civil trial—An action that seeks to gain compensation from someone who stands accused of violating another person's civil rights.

compensatory damages—Money awarded to the winner of a civil law suit to "compensate" him or her for the cost of damages caused by the defendant.

criminal trial—An action that seeks to punish someone accused of a crime.

criminologist—A police scientist who gathers clues and evidence from a crime scene, and later analyzes the evidence.

defendant—The person being accused of a crime in a court of law.

DNA—The genetic code within all human beings that forms the building blocks of life. Each person's DNA is unique. No two people have the same DNA.

domestic abuse—Physical or emotional injuries inflicted by one member of a couple upon the other.

forensic evidence—Evidence gathered from a murder scene.

plaintiff—The party bringing a legal action against a defendant in a court of law.

polygraph—A machine that measures uncontrollable emotional responses to questions in order to determine if someone is telling the truth.

punitive damages—Money that is awarded to the winning party in a civil law suit.

racism—The belief that one race is better than or superior to other races.

search warrant—A special order issued by a judge authorizing police to search a home or business without the permission of the owner. The search is usually conducted in order to find possible evidence of a crime.

sequester—To isolate the members of a jury in order to keep them away from any and all outside influences that might affect their decision-making abilities.

wrongful-death suit—An action in a court brought against a defendant who, through some action, intended or not, is responsible for the loss of life.

Further Reading

Bugliosi, Vincent. *Outrage: The Five Reasons Why O. J. Simpson Got Away With Murder*. New York: W. W. Norton & Company, 1996.

Clark, Marcia With Teresa Carpenter. *Without a Doubt*. New York: Viking Penguin, 1997.

Darden, Christopher With Jess Walter. *In Contempt*. New York: Harper Collins, 1996.

Dershowitz, Alan M. *Reasonable Doubts*. New York: Simon & Schuster, 1996.

Rantald, M. L. *O. J. Unmasked: The Trial, the Truth, and the Media*. Chicago: Open Court, 1996.

Rice, Earl, Jr. *The O. J. Simpson Trial*. San Diego, Calif.: Lucent Books, 1996.

Spence, Gerry. *O. J.: The Last Word*. Gordonville, Va.: Saint Martin's Press, 1997.

Toobin, Jeffrey. *The Run of His Life: The People vs. O. J. Simpson*. New York: Random House, 1996.

Internet Addresses

Court TV Case Files: California v. Simpson

<http://www.courttv.com/verdicts/simpson.html>

Court TV Case Files: Week by Week in the O. J. Simpson Criminal Trial

<http://www.courttv.com/casefiles/simpson/criminal/summary/>

Famous American Trials—University of Missouri at Kansas City Law School: The O.J. Simpson Trial, 1995

<http://www.law.umkc.edu/faculty/projects/ftrials/Simpson/simpson.htm>

Index